Made in God's Image?

CALIFORNIA STUDIES IN THE HISTORY OF ART

Walter Horn, *Founding Editor*
James Marrow, *General Editor*

DISCOVERY SERIES

ABOUT THE DISCOVERY SERIES

Innovative and generously illustrated, books in the
Discovery Series focus on a single important work of art,
artist, or theme in the history of art. Each is distinctive for
the richness of detail and insight it conveys in a concise
format, and each is written in prose that appeals to both
specialists and general readers.

PENNY HOWELL JOLLY

Made in God's Image?

*Eve and Adam in the Genesis Mosaics
at San Marco, Venice*

UNIVERSITY OF CALIFORNIA PRESS

BERKELEY   LOS ANGELES   LONDON

The publisher gratefully acknowledges the contribution provided by the Art Book Fund of the Associates of the University of California Press, which is supported by a major gift from the Ahmanson Foundation.

University of California Press
Berkeley and Los Angeles, California

University of California Press, Ltd.
London, England

© 1997 by
The Regents of the University of California
Library of Congress Cataloging-in-Publication Data
Jolly, Penny Howell.
  Made in God's image? : Eve and Adam in the Genesis mosaics at San Marco,
  Venice / Penny Howell Jolly.
    p.   cm. — (California studies in the history of art.
  Discovery series ; 4)
    Includes bibliographical references and index.
    ISBN 0-520-20537-5 (alk. paper)
    1. Mosaics, Medieval—Italy—Venice.   2. Mosaics, Italian—Italy—Venice.
  3. Bible. O.T. Genesis—Illustrations.   4. Adam (Biblical figure)—Art.   5. Eve
  (Biblical figure)—Art.   I. Title.   II. Series.
  NA3790.J66 1997
  738.52′0945′31—dc20   96-28461
                                                                  CIP

Printed in the United States of America
9 8 7 6 5 4 3 2 1

to Eves and Adams past and present,
especially my parents, Mildred and William Howell,
and my children, Jennifer and Joseph Jolly

Contents

Illustrations

Figures

Acknowledgments

Skidmore College has provided funding that assisted me in traveling and researching in Europe and the United States, as well as contributed toward the purchase of the photographs, for all of which I am grateful. Various friends offered scholarly advice and assistance, including Michael Arnush, Terence Diggory, Kate Greenspan, and Julie Harris; Terri Brandt helped with the final typing. My hearty thanks also go to the editor of this series, James Marrow of Princeton University, and to the staff at the University of California Press, particularly Deborah Kirshman, Fine Arts Editor. Most especially I am indebted to my husband, Jay Rogoff, without whose unfailing enthusiasm and sharp-eyed editing this book would not have been written.

CHAPTER ONE

Introduction

Modern visitors who enter San Marco discover walls and domes covered with mosaics. They are visually exhilarating to experience, particularly because of their brilliant colors and pervasive gold; in terms of their meaning, however, they usually remain less satisfying. Whether because of the difficulty of viewing scenes located high in the vaults or our ignorance of medieval saints' lives, often our only way of answering the question, "What do these mosaics mean?" is to read a guidebook.

However, those of us who stand in the more intimately scaled narthex or atrium, the entryway of the church, and study the mosaic scenes in the southernmost dome (Plate 1) will be rewarded for our efforts. Male and female nudes, prominent trees, a serpent, and cosmic bodies—these are clearly players and props from the well-known story of Creation found in Genesis (see Excerpts). We modern viewers, like our thirteenth-century counterparts who first scrutinized these mosaics, recall the essential story line: God's creation of a blissful golden age, lost to future humans as punishment for the first couple's disobedience. Even though we all know the plot, we are drawn to "read" it one more time, revalidating our recollection of the story. Yet as we scrutinize these mosaics, episode by episode, questions arise. Why does God stand stiffly at the left in so many of the scenes and gesture with his hand? Why are some of the trees blue? These questions reveal one of the reasons for the longevity of this seemingly timeless myth. While on the one hand the numerous retellings retain universal elements, consistent over almost three millennia, on the other hand each retelling is a unique revision. The story's agelessness, then, is due partly to the comforting repetition of traditional elements and partly to its seemingly infinite flexibility as it is adapted to changing religious and social demands of different epochs. Whether Milton or Michelangelo, Augustine or Blake, each re-creator of the myth revises and customizes the narrative to meet the needs of his or her historical situation. Thus the mosaics at San Marco, even though they repeat an old tale, also reflect the specific historical, political, and religious community of thirteenth-century Venice. That this particular retelling was deemed urgent to that community is indicated by the prominence and visibility of these mosaics in the entryway of the city's most important public building. Poor and rich, women and men, laity and clergy alike were to read this new account of the Genesis story because it was relevant to their late medieval lives.

My own fascination with these mosaics grew out of what seemed to me a startling revision in the scene of the labors of Adam and Eve (Plate 2). In that scene, Eve is a paradoxical figure, for she appears glorified at the very moment of her banishment and shame. Unlike similar images of Eve at her labors, where she traditionally sits nursing, this Eve is well-dressed, enthroned, and located more centrally than her bent-over, hard-laboring mate. Childless and idle, she sits with distaff and spindle in her right hand, but these resemble regal attributes more than implements of work: indeed, she is the only figure besides the Creator to appear enthroned in the entire cupola. It is improbable that this image anticipates modern feminist reinterpretations of the Genesis text, where Eve represents the crowning achievement of God's Creation, the heroine who willingly assumes risks in order to obtain divine knowledge.[1] Rather, this radically reimagined scene must be viewed in light of the well-known strains of misogyny and dualism of thirteenth-century Christian thought, according to which Eve typically functions as a negative counterpoint to Adam and as an antitype for Mary, used for contrast rather than similarity.

The novelty of this image is no small matter, since no narrative, textual or visual, would have been better known in thirteenth-century Venice than that of Adam and Eve. Not only does its text form the opening chapters of Genesis and the Old Testament, where it was the subject of both Jewish and Christian exegetes from Philo and Origen to Maimonides and Aquinas, but it was also rewritten and expanded in apocryphal texts. Such elaborations of the story include both Greek and Latin versions of the life of Adam and Eve, further copied and reworked throughout the Middle Ages.[2] The Genesis text figured prominently in the preparations for Lent, the season of penance, and also provided the subject of one of the earliest vernacular mystery plays, the twelfth-century Anglo-Norman *Mystère d'Adam*. World chronicles began with the Creation story, treatises on the Virtues and Vices explained why our first parents failed, and churches were lined with frescoes and mosaics relating the tale.

It is easy to understand why this popular story was told and retold throughout the Middle Ages and re-presented one more time here in Venice. Like most creation myths, its function is etiological, for the narrative offers explanations for why men are the heads of families, why snakes crawl on their bellies, and why we all must work and finally die. It also establishes a template for the first alliance between man and woman, thus coming to serve as a paradigm for male-female relationships in Western culture. Adam and Eve are Everyman and Everywoman; their motivations, actions, and penalties are ours. While their history is a cautionary tale of sin and betrayal, it also offers a model for male and female behavior, marriage, and the household. And just as today the debate concerning human nature— including distinctions between males and females, framed in twentieth-century terms of genetics and neurophysiology—has real social, religious, political, and economic consequences, so in late medieval Venice these analyses of Creation and the first man and woman genuinely affected people's daily lives.

Yet while the Genesis narrative answers fundamental questions, any retelling of the tale raises additional ones. If God is the benevolent Creator of all things, where did evil come from? If Adam is made perfect, in the image of the Deity, how could he sin? Is Eve also made in God's image? Why is the Serpent hostile toward Adam and Eve? Each time any of us reads or tells the tale, we rewrite and reinterpret it, answering these or other questions with explanations appropriate to our proper social, religious, and historical context. Even Jerome's Latin Vulgate translation from the original Hebrew subtly and not so subtly altered the text in ways consistent with his personal history and situation; for example, some scholars have uncovered misogynist tendencies in his choice of words.³ Medieval writers and preachers who were unable to change the main elements of the drama—after all, everyone knew them—consciously and unconsciously analyzed the characters of the actors, attributed motivations to them, and filled in story lines where none existed in the original Genesis text. From some we learn that the Serpent *is* Satan, that Adam sinned because he so loved Eve, and that Eve gave in to the Serpent because they looked alike. The San Marco mosaics, situated in a Venice populated with Crusaders and a wealthy citizenry, warn us about, among other things, the nature of Muslim women's morals and confirm the necessity of sumptuary legislation to regulate the clothing of the Venetian population. And finally, additional questions about the text arose as medieval theologians—and artists—attempted to reconcile the two incompatible versions of human creation synthesized in the opening chapters of Genesis, the first (although written later) found in Genesis 1:1–2:3, and the second (written earlier) beginning with Genesis 2:4. Scholars today recognize that two different authors were at work, the so-called Priestly author (of the P text), working in the sixth century B.C.E., and the mid-tenth-century B.C.E. Yahwist writer (of the J text). In the medieval period, however, Moses was understood to be the single author, and his text needed to be explained as one seamless creation story, inconsistent though it was. Thus, the Genesis story, from J text to P text and their eventual synthesis, to translations from Hebrew to Latin, to multiple written and visual reworkings, is transformed with each retelling, the San Marco mosaics contributing to this palimpsest of meaning and explanation.

The continual retelling of the Genesis myth suggested to me that one significant way of exploring meaning in the San Marco mosaics, the central concern of this book, is by analyzing them as a revision of an established tale, thus revealing their late medieval content through the establishment of difference. This approach is particularly useful here because art historians have identified a group of closely related images of the Genesis story that includes the San Marco mosaics; to some degree, then, art-historical scholarship has emphasized similarities within the group.⁴ My premise, by contrast, is to discern the thirteenth-century alterations and analyze the intentions behind them. As but one in a long line of revisions of the story of Creation, the narrative presented at San Marco offers a singular understanding and vision of divine purpose and human history. Which questions arose from the narrative to interest the thirteenth-century Venetian creators, and which answers seemed most viable to them, inform our understanding of their society. We recognize, then, that the San Marco Creation mosaics form a unique, primary Gothic "text" that can be read and interpreted by modern viewers just as a thirteenth-century Venetian homily would be. No one doubts that Peter Comestor's popular twelfth-century rewriting of the Genesis myth, the *Historia scholastica*,[5] can be analyzed today in terms of how it represents a synthesis of earlier versions of the story, both verbal and visual, nor that it can also be investigated with regard to late-twelfth-century attitudes and mores, different from those of its sources. The same is true, of course, for the mosaics in San Marco. Thus, rather than lamenting the scarcity of texts concerning relations between the sexes and the lack of information on public preaching in thirteenth-century Venice, scholars should recognize that these mosaics can themselves enlighten us with regard to these matters.[6]

A related goal of this book is to consider how visual narratives mean. The mosaicists at San Marco transformed manuscript illuminations intended for a private, literate reader/viewer into monumental, public images for a largely *verbally illiterate* but *visually literate* audience standing within the entry of the most important civic and religious building in Venice; the new location and enlarged scale reinforce the authority of the myth. The fact that it is a narrative further assures viewers that their study will be rewarded by a story that presents order and purpose, cause and effect. While an examination of the "narrative" of one's daily life may reveal only chaos and apparent randomness, when one reads a mosaic cycle one expects to find meaning and purpose, patterns of behavior and significance. On the one hand, viewers already know the story and re-experience it synchronically; seeing the beginning, they anticipate the end, and a glance at the image of the Fall simultaneously evokes nostalgia for the loss of Paradise and dread of the punishments of the earthly realm. On the other hand, the mosaicists have both symbolically and physically shaped their vision of Creation on the ceiling of the narthex, moving from left to right and top to bottom, carefully creating a higher order of existence for

viewers to re-experience diachronically within the real time of their scrutiny. Thus the well-planned structure of the narrative, varying the number
of episodes for different parts of the tale, controls the speed of the viewer's
reading, and the mosaicists consciously introduced into the earliest scenes
in the cycle explanations for and anticipations of its eventual resolution.
What appears a simple relating of a familiar story becomes, in the hands
of the thirteenth-century artist-interpreters, a setting for what Mieke Bal
refers to as the "retrospective fallacy," where a predetermined conclusion
regarding the essential nature of a character colors the entire retelling of
the tale.[7] This retrospective fallacy controls the visual language of the mosaics, encouraging the establishment of patterns and the recognition of
cause and effect.

I am asking the reader of this book to read these visual scenes as though
they are a text; therefore, other considerations for this study are the nature
of visual language—as opposed to verbal language—and the kinds of questions and answers it can pose. A careful explanation and analysis of the
syntax of the visual language used at San Marco, alongside scrutiny of the
textual and visual traditions consulted by the artists, reveal ways in which
meaning is created specifically in the visual arts. Some scholars, questioning whether we can actually read images as we read words, have generally
depended on verbal texts in their analyses of the visual arts.[8] By contrast, I
advance the San Marco Creation cycle as an independent and legible text,
a kind of visual gloss to earlier presentations of the Genesis story, and one
that is still a good read for the modern viewer. I recognize that some kinds
of information may be more accurately and efficiently communicated via
the word, and certainly the Christian Middle Ages esteemed the word and
imputed great authority to it. Yet the image, too, communicates forcefully,
and only partly due to the power of aesthetic response. The visual expres-
sion of relationships of "likeness" and "difference," for example, can be
immediate; in the Genesis tale, it would be difficult for an artist to avoid
the question of exactly *who* was made in the image of the Deity. Further,
that images may be more susceptible to multivalent readings than words
need not be seen as a weakness. The very ability of visual forms to recall a
rich variety of references is one source of their power. As Michael Camille
has explained, a powerful image "need not have one univocal meaning or
one single text that explains it. Rather, it is crucial in propaganda that it
have enough breadth of reference to be read by diverse groups in society."[9] And the San Marco cupola is dealing in powerful propaganda.

When finished with our reading of the mosaics, we shall see that, going well beyond what the Genesis Vulgate text says about Eve and Adam, the mosaicists use visual conventions to depict Eve that deny her visual affinity with the Creator and Adam; she is not fully in the image of God. While it is not surprising that an essential misogyny underlies the mosaics, the pervasiveness of it in the visual language is startling. The San Marco mosaics, by their overall arrangement in the vault of the atrium, by their compositional schema, by the postures of the protagonists, and by multiple details found in the individual scenes, establish Eve as the culpable character from the very moment of her creation in Paradise and depict her as dangerous and unrepentant at the end. Adam is not exonerated from culpability and in a sense falls farther because of his initial closeness to God, yet visually he remains more redeemable. The prelapsarian Adam and Eve at San Marco, created by a process of separation into unequal parts, exist in opposition to one another, and the entire cycle implies the inevitability of Eve's capitulation to sin.

We do not know who was ultimately responsible for the theological positions taken in the mosaics. As Otto Demus has written about thirteenth-century Venice, there is an "almost complete lack of statements on spiritual or even religious matters, a lack that is characteristic of Venice in almost every age." [10] The Procurator of Venice was in charge of all the decoration of San Marco, including seemingly minor details regarding the mosaics, and certainly he was officially responsible. [11] Yet no one knows which theological advisors worked on the project with him, or who provided the single most important visual model, the Cotton Genesis. I shall refer repeatedly to "the mosaicists," even though these were only craft laborers who would have worked from designs decided by the head of the shop, in consultation with appropriate but as yet unidentified civic and/or religious advisors. But, as we shall see as we examine the narrative sequence scene by scene, whoever the creators of this program were, they knew well the syntax of medieval art and used it effectively to warn the citizens of Venice about the ever-present power of women.

CHAPTER TWO

Creation before Eve

The Adam and Eve mosaics, in the first small cupola of the narthex of San Marco in Venice (Plate 1), begin the Old Testament narrative with the story of Creation; lining the upper walls and vaults of the remainder of the narthex are depictions of the subsequent narratives of Noah, Abraham, Joseph, and Moses. The identities of the mosaicists are unknown, but they were probably Western artists who began work in the 1220s and were still working on the extensive cycle in the 1290s.[1] This first cupola, divided into twenty-four frames and arranged in three concentric registers, relates the story of Creation from the *Spirit above the Waters* on the topmost register to the *Labors of Adam and Eve* on the lowest. The narrative then continues on the east lunette with the *Conception of Cain*, a scene directly aligned with the first scenes of each register in the cupola above (Fig. 1), and the *Birth of Abel* (Fig. 2), while the south lunette concludes their story (Fig. 3). Johan Jakob Tikkanen was the first to recognize a relationship between the mosaics and the miniatures of the Cotton Genesis, a manuscript illuminated most likely in Alexandria in the later fifth century, but which burned in 1731.[2] Scholars now generally accept that this manuscript served as the primary visual model for the mosaic cycle.

How Do We Read It? Establishing a Syntax of Visual Language

As we enter through the right door of the west facade into the atrium, the pictorial cycle begins directly before us in the uppermost register of the dome. An abbreviated Latin text, legible from the floor below, appears above each register of scenes, paralleling the visual narrative. The text above the first half of the cycle comes directly from the Vulgate, although in much abbreviated form, while that above the second half is a newly generated text.[3] Yet the text is secondary to the pictorial scenes: although few medieval viewers could read Latin, almost all knew the story of Genesis and would have had no trouble finding the visual start of the cycle.[4] Tracing its easy movement from left to right and down from register to register would not be preconditioned in most cases by the viewers' abilities to read text on a page, but rather by their familiarity with the scenes and figures depicted. Even the angel-day personifications—one angel for the first day of Creation, two for the second, and so forth—lead the viewer, their vertical stances like the strokes of Roman numerals. Thus a visual reading pattern is established: we move from left to right and from top to bottom.

This overall pattern of movement is, of course, meaningful, for in following its unfolding we repeat the significant action of the story. It is a fall, and so, like our first parents, we descend the levels of the dome, from the more divine realm of gold above, to the darker and more mundane world of the lowest register. The first register of Creation relates the incidents of the first three days (Light and Darkness are separated; air and water are distinguished from the firmament; land emerges from the seas), and the second register includes parallel elaborations of those three in days four through six (creation of the sun and moon; of birds and marine creatures; of land creatures and Adam).[5] It is not coincidental that the lowest register is reserved for the creation of woman and the subsequent scenes of temptation, sin, punishment, and expulsion, all shown against a dark green foliage absent from the earlier, higher scenes. The depiction of Adam and Eve in bed actually conceiving Cain—an unfortunate event in human

FIGURE I.

Detail of the Creation
cupola and *Conception
of Cain* in east
lunette,
thirteenth century,
San Marco, Venice.

FIGURE 2.

East lunette, below the
Creation cupola, with
the *Conception of Cain*
and *Birth of Abel*, San
Marco, Venice.

history, rarely depicted in any cycle—and the birth of his brother Abel,
are reserved for an even lower location in the east lunette below and con-
clude the story of the first couple.

The movement from left to right is also significant, for it helps to privilege via primacy the left side of the image (also called the *picture's right*,
or the right side of the image from the vantage of the figures in the scene,
a term used frequently in this book), a compositional device common in
medieval art. Thus, superimposed on the left-to-right narrative movement is a traditional hierarchical system that values centrality and frontal
views and honors the picture's right over its left.[6] The mosaicists used
these devices knowingly and consistently to imbue their compositions with
meaning.

Figural postures in these mosaics are neither generally expressive nor
particularly naturalistic; rather, the poses are conventionalized and repeti-
tive and must be understood within a medieval context wherein gestures

FIGURE 3.

South lunette, below
the Creation cupola,
with the *Story of Cain
and Abel*, San Marco,
Venice.

had legal power and written documents were often suspect.[7] Semiotic studies of gestures in the medieval world confirm that artists created systems of conventional gestures to express intended meaning.[8] Some gestures were more closely based on observed human body language, whether found in daily life—for example, those in the art of Giotto in the early fourteenth century—or in highly conventionalized ecclesiastical or court rituals. Others, like the *adlocutio*, or speaking, gesture in classical art (raised right hand), became conventions and were widely known to a variety of audiences over centuries. However, the premise for all of them is the same and helps to explain the almost obsessive interest in the state of one's body in medieval monasticism: the body on the exterior is a direct reflection of the soul on the interior. Whether one were a simple sinner or possessed by the Devil, this would be revealed through appearance, specifically through posture. Although symbolic gestures in art were not necessarily mimetic of those in life, medieval audiences—like our image-oriented culture today—were visually sophisticated in their understanding of these conventionalized postures and their moral implications. Viewers who were verbally illiterate could nonetheless recognize standard postures and arrangements of figures, and their visual memories would have been trained to note echoes of these in later episodes within a narrative, establishing what could be called visual "similes" and "metaphors." The San Marco mosaics depend on exactly these skills of visual memory, of noticing similes and metaphors, and on understanding symbolic gestures and conventions.

The Omnipotent Deity

The first nine scenes concern the story of God and Creation prior to the making of Adam. The central questions posed here concern the nature of the Deity himself and the origin of evil. Discussion regarding God's nature arose from chapters 1–3 in the Genesis text itself, particularly because of the inconsistencies in the P and J versions. The P text (Gen. 1:1–2:3) characterizes an ideal and clearly benevolent Creator, omnipotent and omniscient, who generously forms a creature in his own image. This is the God who but speaks in order to create, confirms "that it was good," and blesses the creatures he makes. There exists also in the P text a sense of hierarchy in the world order, established by the formulaic movement from Day One through Day Seven, and by the command that the final creature made on Day Six will "have dominion over the fishes of the sea, and the fowls of the air, and the beasts, and the whole earth, and every creeping creature that moveth upon the earth" (Gen. 1:26). Yet this being seems irreconcilable with the J-text Deity who appears in the second, nonhierarchical account of Creation that begins in Genesis 2:4: a more human and inept God, whose inability to control his creatures challenges his omnipotence, and whose need to search among the animals for a proper helper for Adam and to call into the bushes after the hiding Adam and Eve seems to confirm his lack of omniscience. A further complication arises from the juxtaposition of the P and J deities: how could the all-controlling and benevolent Creator of the P text deny Adam and Eve access to the Tree of Knowledge of Good and Evil, if that knowledge were good for them? And if the knowledge were not good, but evil, why would he have created it? The Cotton Genesis, the profusely illustrated and unabridged manuscript that was used as a model by the mosaicists, offers illuminations of both the P and the J versions. The artists of the San Marco mosaics, however, revised and eliminated parts of its narrative in favor of a more consistent and unified interpretation of the story. Their cycle depicts the powerful God of the P text yet offers a plausible explanation for the origins of evil from the J narrative.

Creation before Adam

Typical of medieval Creation cycles, San Marco's opens with the P text of chapter 1. Given that the remainder of the scenes will methodically move from left to right, it is telling that the *Spirit above the Waters* (Plate 1, immediately below the central roundel) begins the sequence with a back-and-forth movement created by the lines of the amorphous waters below and behind the dove, while the dove itself seems to hover and move up and to the left. As yet there is no order or direction to Creation, and the composition reveals this chaos and timelessness. But the following scene, the *Separation of Light from Darkness* (Plate 3), is one of the most important in the series, for it immediately establishes conventions and hierarchical formulas used throughout the rest of the cycle.

Inspired by the P text, the mosaicists stand the omnipotent Creator at the left, the picture's right, in anthropomorphic form. He is the traditional Christ Logos—the Word Incarnate—of John 1:1, who holds a cross-scepter in his veiled left hand, wears a cruciform halo around his head, and raises his right hand in a gesture of both speech and action: "And God said: Be light made" (Gen. 1:3).[9] In the San Marco mosaics, this use of the Roman *adlocutio* gesture of a raised right hand, whether pointing with one finger, with two fingers extended, or open-palmed, generally indicates a spoken text from the Vulgate, cued there by the *dixit* or *ait* formula, "he said." The Creator also consistently uses his right hand to gesture and speak, clearly the proper way, as confirmed by the *Tower of Babel* (Fig. 4) mosaic in the nearby barrel vault in which the confusion of languages of Genesis 11 is expressed visually by the variety of right- and left-handed speaking gestures used by members of the crowd. Elsewhere in the mosaics, left-hand gestures indicate duplicity, spoken anger, or an admonition.[10] The few exceptional uses of left hands in this first cupola will be noted below.

In the Creation cupola, this preferred posture for the Creator is an ideological stance, representing authority and control. The Creator appears twenty times in the cupola; of these, he appears fifteen times at the picture's right (our left), in the position of primacy in terms of the left-to-right syntax (in one of these his posture parallels that of Adam, who stands further to the picture's right), gesturing toward the unfolding scene (e.g., Plates 3, 4, and 5, Figs. 5 and 7). In these, he functions as what I will call

FIGURE 4.

Tower of Babel, west half of north vault, San Marco, Venice.

the *active agent*, the Creator who speaks by gesturing with his right hand, who thereby brings into being the objects of Creation and who directs the ongoing action of the universe.[11] The very repetition of this commanding figure helps to move the cycle from scene to scene, echoing the anaphora of the textual formula, "And God said." Any break in this pattern, of course, signals us to take careful note. We shall see below the significance of the three times that he is depicted as a more static, central figure in the scene (see Figs. 9, 25, and 26), as well as of the two highly unusual scenes where the mosaicists reverse the Creator so he stands to the picture's left, facing to our left (Plate 6 and left half of Plate 7). Particularly because these latter two postures are purposeful changes from the Cotton Genesis model, they carry significance.

The *Separation of Light and Darkness* (Plate 3) presents the first in a series of binaries and clarifies the method of creation God uses to establish them. Here the Creator separates two formerly unified things into opposing positive and privative elements, Light and the absence of all light, Darkness.[12] In the mosaic, we see the personification of the first day of Creation in the form of an angel with raised arms, who rises behind three concentric red circles representing Light and reaches its left arm into the shadows above the blue circles of Darkness. Deprived of light, the left arm and wing become totally blue; unusual in medieval art, the angel has become distinctly bicolored.

Augustine's ideas regarding Creation, pervasive throughout the Middle Ages but perhaps of special interest in thirteenth-century Venice,[13] influenced the San Marco mosaicists. For example, the presence of a single angelic form on the first day, succeeded by a pair for the second, a trio for the third, and so on, refers to Augustine's nontemporal understanding of the six days of Creation as angelic knowledge (in his *De Genesi ad litteram*).[14] Not creators themselves, as some would have it, they instead observe God's Creation, receiving knowledge of all things created.

In his *City of God* (11.9), Augustine has additional ideas about the angels that are relevant to the San Marco *Separation of Light and Darkness* and thirteenth-century Venice. He identifies them with "heaven" and the "light which was called 'Day'" of Genesis 1:1 and 1:3–5 but also asserts that their division into two communities—the good and the bad, or the enlightened and unenlightened—occurred on this very first day of Creation, when God separated Light from Darkness (11.19). By the thirteenth century a variety of traditions existed regarding exactly when the good angels and fallen angels, led by the Archangel Michael and Lucifer, respectively, fought and separated, but the distinctly divided halves of this mosaic and the unusual bicoloration of the angel suggest that the San Marco mosaicists take this Augustinian approach to the origin of evil. Evil has already entered the world on the first day.

Questions regarding the source of evil, the nature of God, and the reasons for the Fall loomed large in twelfth- and thirteenth-century Europe, a time when the Manichean-inspired Catharist heresy was rampant in southern France and northern Italy, and explain in part why Augustine's views were so significant at this time. The late medieval Catharists, or Albigensians, identified two creative forces in the world. One was essentially the Old Testament God, benevolent and the source for all good; the other was an equally powerful source of evil. For both the early Manicheans and their later followers, matter was entirely evil, marriage and pregnancy to be condemned, and salvation obtained only when the soul separated from the body. Augustine, who shared the late antique world's suspicion of the body and material desire, walked a very careful line in his defense of monotheism and the physical Creation, but it was he who successfully disputed the Manichean heretics in the late fourth and early fifth centuries with, among others, these very texts.

According to Augustine and reiterated by Aquinas in the later thirteenth century, possibly a few years later than the Genesis mosaics, evil is not the creation of a second being, but rather a privative state: the absence of good.[15] Stating that when God separated Light from Darkness, he also created the good and bad angels, Augustine explains that God permitted evil, not out of ignorance, but because of his wish for there to be free will. Evil, both among the angels and in humans, comes from a spirit that is defective, that is, deprived of knowledge, and finds its roots in pride and envy, sins that bear no relation to the world of matter. The Fourth Lateran Council of 1215—condemning the Cathars' supreme principle of evil—reiterated the orthodox position that evil comes from error, not from matter. "The Devil and the other demons were created by God with a good nature; but they themselves through their own agency became evil."[16] And Augustine had already centuries earlier assured his readers of God's omnipotence: "For He alone could make this discrimination . . . before they fell, to foreknow that they would fall, and that, being deprived of the light of truth, they would abide in the darkness of pride."[17] The lit side of the angel in the San Marco mosaic, near the red light, represents the enlightened angels, while the blue side represents the fallen.[18] Two "equations" are immediately established that will remain valid for the rest of the mosaics:

Light = Red = Good Angels = Picture's Right Side = Truth;
and
Darkness = Blue = Fallen Angels = Picture's Left Side = Pride.

FIGURE 5.
Creation of the Plants,
detail of the Creation
cupola, San Marco,
Venice.

The recurrence of the Creator in the active-agent pose in seven of the first nine scenes establishes a rhythmic sense of the progression of Creation, as does the expanding number of angels who personify the successive days. Each appearance of the Creator corresponds with exactly one speech within the Genesis text (each indicated by *dixit* or *ait:* e.g., Gen. 1:6, 1:9, and 1:11). Possibly the raised hands of the angels refer to the enlightened angels who, according to Augustine, follow the command, "Praise ye Him, all His angels" (*City of God* 11.33), for Genesis 1–3 attributes no speech to the angels. Scenes four and five have no specific text above them and are two of only three scenes to include *tituli* within the pictorial field: TERRAM in the *Separation of the Seas and the Dry Land*, and LIGNV[M] POMI in the *Creation of the Plants* (Fig. 5). In a change from the more extensively vegetated scene in the Cotton Genesis, the artist of this latter scene includes only a few fernlike plants on the grassy ground, isolating two large fruit trees against the gold ground and highlighting their fruit with glistening white tesserae.[19] Thus, our attention is drawn to the earth, rather than the seas separated from it, and to the fruit trees, key elements for viewers well aware of future events.

The second register begins with the *Creation of the Heavenly Bodies* (see Plate 4), and the viewer is reminded of various of the opposing dualities as the red sun—associated with Light, the day, and the obedient angels—is to the picture's upper right, close to the Creator, while the blue moon—associated with Darkness, the night, and Lucifer—rests in a less honored part of the starry firmament, to the picture's bottom left. The Venetians' knowledge and love of the sea are reflected in the detail of the *Creation of the Birds and Marine Creatures* (Fig. 6),[20] a scene that reinforces the ideas of separation and opposition by the strict segregation of air and water creatures into distinct halves of the composition, followed by their blessing (see Plate 5). There God exhorts them to "increase and multiply" (Gen. 1:22), so his figure reappears with outstretched hand indicating speech, rather than a specific gesture of blessing. The creatures are shown as overlapping pairs of males and females, an invention of the thirteenth-century artists[21] and apparently a response to God's procreation command. These creatures seem to share a single body with two heads, creating a sense of visual unity and stressing the concept of coming together rather than that of separation and difference. The paired animals in the following *Creation of the Terrestrial Animals* (Fig. 7) similarly demonstrate unity between the sexes and stress via their matched appearances the appropriateness of their pairing, even though the Genesis text makes no mention of males and females, or even of multiplying.

Yet within this visual message of coupling, a singular animal is included, a serpent beneath the feet of the angels in the *Blessing* (see Plate 5). This creature lies at the center of a vertical axis that visually explains the origin of sin and the Serpent's pivotal role. This axis is formed when viewers below the cupola read images sequentially that are vertically proximate due to the registration, but narratively distant. This method of encouraging visual comparison, not available within the linear format of a manuscript like the Cotton Genesis, is a possibility within the cupola design, enhanced by the curved shape of the dome. Thus the Serpent's body in the *Blessing* lies below the blue Darkness, where Lucifer was created in the register above, and above the scene wherein he first appears in the narrative, the

Temptation of Eve (see Plate 1). His head rests immediately above the word "DECIPIT" ("deceives") in the *titulus* for that last-named scene. Compositionally the mosaicists created visual patterns of relationships, anticipating from the beginning what the final consequences will be. They also assure us that the Cathars are wrong; we see that the benevolent Deity created this Serpent in a state of innocence, even blessed him, and yet—through free will, as Augustine established centuries earlier—he became the agent of proud Lucifer and deceived Eve.

Made in God's Image: Adam

The *Forming of Adam* (Fig. 8) is remarkable in its depiction of a single male human, because the singular form again contrasts with the mostly paired creatures who came before him. It also offers a clarifying visual gloss to a historically ambiguous section of the Vulgate, which describes a paired, two-sexed creature: "So God created a human in his own image, in the image of God he created him; male and female he created them." This famous "first" Creation of Genesis 1:27, by the P author, is ambiguous in Latin but clearer in the Hebrew and has been discussed at length by rabbis, theologians, and scholars for more than two thousand years. This is not the place to reproduce those many arguments, but to note two facts about the text. First, both the Hebrew and Latin texts for Genesis 1:27 use a term indicating a singular human creature, with no reference to sex (*adam* and *homo*), but then immediately refer in the plural to a male and a female. Second, whether this creature is singular or plural, without sex or bisexual, *it* is what is made in the image of the Deity, and this is never said about the creatures in the second Genesis Creation.[22]

The mosaicists of San Marco, faced with the problem of a missing folio in their model and an ambiguous text, avoided depicting either an unsexed human or a two-sexed creature, even while using an abbreviated inscription from Genesis 1:27 above their mosaic. This *titulus* omits any reference to difference ("male and female"), stressing instead the unity between the Deity and the creature: "FACIAMVS HOMINEM AD IMAGINEM ET SIMILITVDINEM NOSTRAM" (Let us make a human in our image and likeness). For their visual model, they turned to a later folio in the Cotton Genesis, for, like many artists before and after them, they chose to envision the less ambiguous text of the J Creation of Genesis 2:7 and 2:22, which they

FIGURE 8.
Forming of Adam, detail
of the Creation cupola,
San Marco, Venice.

interpreted as indicating a male figure made first, from clay, followed by the separation of a woman from his side.[23] Thus the mosaicists, retaining the text and narrative location of Genesis 1:27, chose to ignore any sexual ambiguity implied in either account of Creation and insisted that the figure made in the image of the Deity was a single male figure formed from the clay of the earth.

The scene of Adam's forming is barren, for according to the second Genesis account, the body is made from clay prior to the planting of Eden in the east. The Genesis text includes no speech by God preceded by the *dixit* or *ait* formula, and so the Creator here does not gesture to speak but instead works with two hands to form the right arm of Adam. This is the first time we have seen the Deity as physically active, working by material action rather than by verbal command. This may explain why the Creator is seated on a golden, jeweled throne: the action of forming Adam from clay is so mundane and humble—in Hebrew, the verb used is a potter's

term; in Latin, the simple *formavit*—that the artists feel the need to reassure the viewer that this is still the regal Lord God of Heaven.

Seemingly out of place, but textually in sequence following the Genesis 1:27 account of Creation, the *Blessing of the Seventh Day* interposes itself between the forming and the animation of Adam (see Plate 1; Fig. 9). Lacking the *dixit* or *ait* formula, the Creator does not speak with his right hand but lays it on the head of the personified seventh day, blessing it before the other six. Again the Creator is enthroned, but this time the composition is governed by a hierarchical style and is symmetrical, static, and frozen in time. The Cotton Genesis miniature did not follow this format,[24] but the thirteenth-century artist, sensitive to the meaning of the scene, recalls that God's resting on the seventh day was the cause of the blessing and evokes this "resting" compositionally. However, this is no human in repose—he is not limp or obviously tired—but a Deity majestically enthroned. Once again, the visual syntax tells us how to read the

FIGURE 9.

Blessing of the Seventh Day, detail of the Creation cupola, San Marco, Venice.

scenes, for, for the first time since Creation began, the viewer is not rushed along from left to right but stops before the centralized and frontal Deity, as though finally a punctuational period were depicted in the visual text.

The *Animation of Adam* (see Plate 6), where God gives to Adam his *animus* or soul in the form of a psyche, awkwardly rekindles the narrative by placing Adam in the first position in the composition and reverses the figure of the Deity in the second position, to the picture's left. Compositionally this is one of the most remarkable scenes in the series, because it abruptly interrupts and then redirects the narrative flow, causing it now to move from the viewer's right to left. At the same moment that the Genesis text suddenly shifts to the J section, seemingly repeating itself with a second account of Creation, so do the mosaicists reverse the flow, returning the viewer to the earlier forming and speeding up the tempo.[25] The reversed position of this unusually active and energetic Deity (he again does not speak) encourages our eyes to run back across the symmetrical *Blessing* to the *Forming of Adam,* and then return to the *Animation.* We are reminded emphatically that only when Adam receives his soul has he become fully "like" God. The phrase "in the image" was certainly understood in the Middle Ages as a reference, not to Adam's physicality—even though images express this idea in *physical* likeness—but to Adam's rational soul.[26] No longer clay-colored and small, he now stands erect and in the position usually occupied by the Creator. The mosaicists have substituted a dualist, two-stage creation for the original four scenes of Adam's creation in the Cotton Genesis,[27] thus highlighting only two events—the making first of Adam's body and then of his soul. The reversal of the latter composition signals that we are to review this section of the narrative, for the moments of God's forming of Adam's body and his gift of a soul are high points of God's Creation.

The mosaicists' consistent use of a visual syntax clarifies the ambiguity of the Genesis 1:27 text by demonstrating Adam's similarity to God. Of Adam's fifteen appearances in the cycle, he stands four times in the active-agent pose at the picture's right; two other times he parallels the Creator in God's typical pose and appears next to him, second in the scene, and still at the picture's right; another two times, in compositions where the Creator is frontal and centralized, Adam is again at the picture's (and God's) honored right side; and an additional two times Adam appears at the center, closer than Eve to the Creator at the picture's right. In only

three scenes is he distinctly at the picture's left: at the fateful moment when
he first meets Eve and calls her "Woman" (see Fig. 19); when he takes the
fruit from Eve and sins (see Fig. 20); and when he labors after his Fall (see
Plate 2). Eve's postures, as we will see, are so unlike the Creator's that the
mosaicists' visual answer to the textually generated question, "Who was
made in the image of God?" is clear from the very beginning: Adam, but
certainly not Eve.

The second register ends with another gift from God to the first man,
his introduction into the bucolic Garden of Paradise (Fig. 10). With his
right hand, God pulls Adam through the clearly labeled *Porta Paradisi* into
his lush Garden and, with his left, gestures toward the two prominent trees.
Adam is again granted the honored first position in the composition, but
God acts as his guide, eagerly leading him forward, their two figures moving
parallel to each other. The trees are those of Life and of Knowledge, located

FIGURE 10.

*Introduction of Adam
into Paradise*, detail of
the Creation cupola,
San Marco, Venice.

at the center of Paradise, and the four personifications of the Rivers of Paradise appropriately lie beneath them.

The first tree is certainly the Tree of Life.[28] Honored by its compositionally more central position and proximity to the Deity, this tree remains consistent in form throughout the mosaics (compare Plates 2 and 7 and Fig. 24). It is ironic, but not unusual in medieval art, that the form of the more dangerous tree, the one that needed above all else to be identified by our first parents, changes throughout the cycle. It is first alluded to by the two apple trees in the upper register's *Creation of the Plants* (see Fig. 5); it reappears three times in later scenes with striking blue foliage, although each time varying slightly (see Plates 7 and 11 and Fig. 24); and when Eve finally plucks the fruit, it is botanically identifiable as a fig tree (see Fig. 20). Here, in Adam's introduction into Eden, it is a relatively undistinguished green tree. Yet its sinister quality is suggested by the mosaicists' prominent inclusion of left-handed gestures. In an almost certain thirteenth-century alteration of the model, the four river personifications raise their left hands and point toward the Tree of Knowledge.[29] More remarkable, however, is God's gesture with his left hand. If, as Weitzmann believes, this is a conflation of two scenes in the Cotton Genesis, the *Introduction* and *God's Admonition to Adam*, then this could be interpreted as a speech gesture referring to Genesis 2:16, where God commands Adam not to eat, for he will die.[30] If so, it is the only time in the Genesis mosaics that God speaks with his left hand. Although the narrative has once again picked up and moves comfortably from left to right, the five gesturing left hands cause the viewer to anticipate well in advance the point in the narrative when that tree will play a sinister role in human destiny. Viewers standing below the cupola are once again encouraged to look for proximities created by the registration of the dome (Fig. 11). Directly above Adam's introduction into Paradise and the admonition is the *Creation of the Plants*, including the first reference to a garden and the Tree of Knowledge, while directly below is the *Expulsion*, where Adam and Eve are finally expelled from that same garden.

FIGURE 11.

Northeast corner of
the Creation cupola,
showing vertical align-
ment of scenes, San
Marco, Venice.

CHAPTER THREE

Maid in God's Image?

Eve as the Embodiment of Difference

The first scene of the lowest register, the *Naming of the Animals* (Fig. 12), begins the tale of Eve. God's right hand, gesturing a *dixit* speech, states that it is not good for the human (*homo*) to be alone. And so the search begins among all the pairs of animals for a suitable mate for the singular human creature, but it ends in failure. The mosaicists reestablish the peaceful and bucolic mood of the Garden of Eden, all the better to remind the viewer of the loss about to occur. For example, as in their Creation scenes above, the paired animals show a remarkable degree of undifferentiated unity between the sexes, each set of creatures once again seeming to be a single body with two heads. From lion—honored here and earlier, probably due to the relation to San Marco[1]—to hedgehog, the creatures loll in the paradisal setting, while Adam touches with his left hand one head of the lion pair and, his right hand raised in speech, grants a name. Symbolic of the extraordinary power and domination of his act, Adam stands in the active-agent pose of the Creator, and the scene recalls the

Creation of the Terrestrial Animals (see Fig. 7) in the previous register; the two scenes are visual similes. Only the slight turn of Adam's head and right foot acknowledge the true seat of his power, the Deity enthroned behind him. Yet with a different sense of hierarchy than that found in the model, the thirteenth-century mosaicists have "bumped" Adam from the first position, retaining it for God.[2] Surely this also explains why God is here seated, another change from the fifth-century model. In a kind of divine one-upmanship, just when Adam becomes like the Creator of the first six days, the Creator himself sits enthroned in regal majesty. Once again the visual syntax leaves no doubt as to the relation between the two similar males. The Deity does not give up his authority here but merely delegates some of it to Adam.

The mosaic's message that Adam is exceptionally powerful and "in the image" of the Deity, and simultaneously different from the paired beasts, concurs with medieval discussions of the significance of Adam's act of naming. The episode was potentially an embarrassing one owing to its unfortunate intimation of ineptness on the part of God and Adam's neediness: why would the omniscient Creator need to hunt—unsuccessfully, no less!—for a mate for Adam? Writers quickly switched the focus of their exegesis to other aspects of Adam's role. The early rabbis, for example, suggested that Adam's naming demonstrated his superiority over the angels, while Augustine emphasized Adam's difference from the animals, created as he was as a singular being with a rational soul far superior to the beasts' (*City of God* 12.21), and thus downplayed Adam's need for a mate.[3] Peter Comestor, in his popular late-twelfth-century expansion of the Genesis text, the *Historia scholastica*, asserts that Adam's prelapsarian superiority is confirmed by two factors. First, he is in God's image, that is, he has a rational soul, and second, God has given him dominion over the animals.[4] The mosaicists orchestrate their scene with similar intention: they visually confirm Adam's godlike perfection and superiority within Eden. Further, for the first time we see Adam act. The question now shifts to the role of Adam's missing helper. What will it be? Why does Adam need a helper? And where will that helper fit within this hierarchy of God-Adam-animals? We shall see that Eve is no side issue when it comes to explanations for the Fall; rather, she embodies difference.

As semiotics reminds us, there is no meaning without difference. If we saw only blue, there could be no such thing as "color"; if there were only

good in the world, we not only would have no concept of "evil" but also could have no concept of "good." Rather than deny Adam's initial perfection, the mosaicists enhance it with Eve's contrasting imperfection, and they will accomplish this in a variety of ways, introducing both iconographic and compositional motifs to demonstrate Eve's "difference" from her ideal mate. This makes Adam's fall, from a greater height, all the more tragic. Eve will also play, of course, a directly causal role in the narrative, explaining how such a divinelike being could be capable of sin.

The Creation of Eve

The next scene, a double one including both the *Taking of the Rib* and the *Forming of Eve* (see Plate 7), is one of the most remarkable and inventive scenes in the cupola. The bucolic Garden of Paradise is replaced by a dark forest, as the openness and prominent gold sky of the previous images are

from now on shaded by dense foliage. Artists frequently indicate a change of scene for Eve's creation; typically, as here, the protagonists enter a more mundane realm, and the Deity takes on more of the characteristics of the earth-inhabiting, J-text personality. In a Parisian manuscript of about 1250 (Plate 8), God the Creator shifts from being outside the circular cosmos as he creates it to inside the pictorial frame when he forms Eve, while Michelangelo's Deity in his Sistine Chapel ceiling flies majestically in the first four scenes of Creation but descends to stand on earth when he calls forth Eve from Adam's side (Fig. 13). Suggestive of the gravity of these events, there is a slowing of narrative pace with the *Taking of the Rib* and the *Forming*; for the first time, a single frame has two distinct episodes within it.

The *Taking of the Rib* immediately establishes Eve's inferior nature, and curiously, to do this, it shows both Adam and God in somewhat debased states. First, the scene breaks with all previous postural conventions

FIGURE 13.

Michelangelo, *Creation of Eve*, detail from the Sistine Chapel ceiling, 1508–12, Rome, The Vatican.

regarding both Adam and the Deity and establishes a sense of reversal. In a deliberate inversion of the probable composition in the Cotton Genesis, Adam rather than God appears first, and his classical posture of sleep, cutting diagonally across the corner of the composition, disrupts the repeated rhythm of vertical stances we have seen thus far. The Creator leans over him, turning to remove the rib, and for the first and only time is in profile—a posture traditionally associated with evil and rarely used for God in medieval art.[5] No longer standing statically or seated majestically, the Deity assumes a very human and momentary posture of movement; the only visual simile within the cupola is that of Adam the sinner, laboring after his expulsion (see Plate 2). The fact that God removes a rib from Adam's left side, rather than the more common—and symbolically positive—right side, is also significant. Typically in thirteenth-century art and theology, the taking of the rib to create Eve and her subsequent marriage to Adam were seen as types for the later creation of Ecclesia from the side wound of the new Adam, Christ, and their union.[6] However, this mosaic expresses a binary opposition between Eve and Ecclesia, for by the later Middle Ages Christ's side wound was well established as being on his right side, while his left side at the Crucifixion was associated with Ecclesia's antagonist, Synagoga. The reversal at San Marco of the positions of God and Adam, a deliberate change from the model and an interruption of the narrative flow, allowed the mosaicist to have God separate a rib from Adam's sinister, left side. Thus Eve is condemned even before her creation.[7] The reversal of the figures further directs the viewer's attention downward, where Adam's left hand seems to clutch the earth from which he was made and where a grapevine grows. The fact that Adam sleeps during the rib removal further damns Eve, for sleep was associated with the abandonment of rational faculties in favor of sensual pursuits.[8] The mosaicists, cognizant of this tradition, take care specifically to remind us of Adam's imperfect state during Eve's "birth" through inclusion of a simile; in the adjacent barrel vault lies the naked and drunken Noah, planter of the grapevine, sleeping in a pose similar to Adam's at Eve's creation (Fig. 14).[9]

The tree that grows behind Adam, as though from his side, is identical in form to the Tree of Life in the Garden above, and both it and the grapevine refer to future events in human history. They are typological references to the death by crucifixion on a tree of the new Adam, Christ, and

to the Eucharist, wherein the body that was sacrificed will save humankind. Thus before the woman is even formed, we are forewarned that she and consequently Adam will sin, necessitating that a new Adam come to save humanity from the folly she initiates. Here lies the old Adam, still immortal. But the soil clenched in his left hand will become accursed, no longer a place of rest but of toil, and his sleep reminds us of his subsequent mortality and return to that same earth he clutches, from which he was made. His burial place, according to legend, will be the eventual site of the Crucifixion, and from either seeds of the Tree of Life or a branch of the Tree of Knowledge planted in his dead remains will grow the tree that will supply the wood of that Cross.[10] By the thirteenth century, both Western and Byzantine images of the Crucifixion show the Tree of Life and/or the Cross growing from the side of a reclining Adam, similes of the posture and tree here, and some examples specifically depict the Fall of Adam and

FIGURE 14.

The Drunkenness and Death of Noah, east half of north vault, San Marco, Venice.

Eve as taking place at the base of that Tree-Cross, establishing clearly the typological links between it and Redemption.[11] But it is quite unusual that at San Marco the earlier scene of Eve's creation—not Adam and Eve's actual sin—is used as the antitype for the Crucifixion. The opposition established here is between two bodies: Eve's, associated with carnality and the sin of the Fall, and Christ's mortified corpus, which will offer redemption through the ritual of the Eucharist.

The second half of the scene depicts the Creator actually "building" Eve, and we now see her for the first time (see Plate 7). It is ironic that both the Hebrew text and the Vulgate following it use architectural terms for the making of Eve (Gen. 2:22), while humble potter's terms were used for Adam, for the mosaicists' visualization of the text does not elevate Eve's formation above Adam's.[12] Once the bent-over Creator removes the rib from Adam at the picture's right, the creation of Eve's body occurs at the picture's left. First stands God, once again erect, forming her shoulder with his right hand while holding her wrist with his left. She turns toward him, also erect, and stares blankly. Her creation, like Adam's, is shown in two parts, but God makes no obvious gesture here of giving her first a body and then a soul.

Demonstrating differences between the creations of God's two creatures was important to medieval theologians, because it helped to establish that, while Adam is made in the image of God, this is not quite the case with Eve.[13] Adam's creation occurs before Eve's and results in a unique being; hers follows his and yields a derivative and even defective creature. Orthodox writers admitted that Eve had a soul, but their discussions all reveal remarkable ambiguity toward women and the body. Augustine, for example, concludes that, while both Adam and Eve were made in the image of God, Adam's soul is superior because it possesses the higher reasoning capabilities of *sapientia*, the ability to understand divine truths. Eve's exhibits inferior capabilities, functioning only on the lower level of *scientia*, or sense perception. For him, Adam is superior and associated with the soul, Eve weaker and associated with the body.[14] Peter Abelard, one of the least misogynist of medieval writers, states first that Adam and Eve were equals prior to the Fall, but then inexplicably accuses Eve of inferior moral judgment, caviling that "man is called His image, but woman only His likeness."[15] Thomas Aquinas, writing about the same time that the narthex mosaics were being worked on and espousing similar ideas, concludes that the female is a defective version of the male, possessing the *imago dei* in an inferior way, and that her secondary creation *from* Adam's body confirms her subordination to man.[16] Nontheological writers applied these ideas to the fields of law and medicine; for example, a thirteenth-century political tract states, "Man is created in God's image, but woman is made in man's image and for that reason are women subject to men by natural law."[17]

While specifics vary from writer to writer, the essential difference with regard to Adam's and Eve's natures lies in the binary opposition of "spiritual" and "carnal." Understanding Eve to be "of the body" is a commonplace in medieval theology and is linked to her later "seduction" of Adam and her role as mother of all humans.[18] At San Marco, this idea is expressed in the Latin text above this scene of her forming, where the word "CARNE[M]" ("flesh") is placed directly above her figure. Only those relatively few who were verbally literate could read it, but it would cue a preacher, for example, to recall Eve's identity with the flesh. But this idea is also expressed visually, for immediately to Eve's left and overlapped by her left arm grows a striking blue tree. The later appearance of the Serpent in this blue tree confirms its connection to Lucifer and the fallen angels from Day One of Creation and to the Tree of Knowledge of Good and Evil, the tree long associated with unenlightenment and carnal and sexual knowledge. Like the nearby Tree of Life next to Adam, it stands appropriately in the middle of the Garden, but its qualities oppose those of the Tree of Life, just as Eve's oppose Adam's.

San Marco owned a relic of the True Cross that was miraculously preserved during a fire in 1231,[19] and probably the veneration of this famous relic inspired the special attention to tree symbolism in the cupola mosaics. The juxtaposition in Eve's *Creation* of two opposed trees—of Life and of Knowledge—reflects popular and well-known thirteenth-century iconographies of paired trees. For example, while Eve is associated with the Tree of Knowledge that brings death, Eve's antitype, Mary, is associated with the Tree of Jesse and the generation of Christ. The pictorial formula for this latter, a prophecy of salvation, includes a prone figure with a tree sprouting from his side, a simile recalled to the visually literate viewer by the sleeping Adam with the Tree of Life.[20] The paired trees in Eden probably allude as well to the Tree of Virtues and the Tree of Vices, another popular allegory (Figs. 15 and 16).[21] These trees bear the old Adam and the new Adam, Christ; the root of the Tree of Vices is Pride, the sin most

FIGURE 15.

Tree of Vices, De fructibus carnis et spiritus,
second quarter twelfth
century, Salzburg,
Universitätsbibliothek,
M I 32, fol. 75v.

commonly recognized as the cause of the Fall, while that of the Tree of
Virtues is Humility. When depicted in manuscripts, the paired trees typically appear on the verso of one side and its adjacent recto; labels on the
two images oppose many of the contraries we have discussed here: *dextera*
and *sinistra,* good and evil, Ecclesia and Synagoga, fruits of the spirit and
fruits of the flesh. Verbal and visual treatments of these trees are many and
varied, but the mosaicists show their knowledge of several of these conventions by their intentional opposition of Adam and the Tree of Life to Eve
and the Tree of Knowledge.

    This message of Eve's inherent inferiority and difference is asserted by
the visual syntax of this two-part scene of her creation, for the composition
and gestures, as well as the iconographic themes, all emphasize Eve's sepa-
rateness from Adam. It is more common among both the Cotton Genesis

FIGURE 16.

Tree of Virtues, De fructibus carnis et spiritus, second quarter twelfth century, Salzburg, Universitätsbibliothek, M I 32, fol. 76r.

recension—other than the Cotton Genesis itself—and other medieval images of Eve's creation to depict a single scene showing her body in the process of emerging from the side of Adam. Why did the mosaicists alter the model by conflating two scenes into a single frame yet retain the model's unusual two-part creation? Their split-yet-combined composition allows these dualities between male and female, Ecclesia and Eve, the Tree of Life and the Tree of Knowledge, to reverberate from side to side of the composition and highlights our sense of Eve's otherness and her separation from Adam. As noted above, the other creatures of God were paired as males and females, with overlapping, unified bodies; their maleness and femaleness were seen as two aspects of the same thing. This symbiosis is avoided visually for Adam and Eve until after they sin, even though the text states that God and Adam are searching for a suitable mate for Adam because he is alone. Had the mosaicists made the more traditional depiction of Eve's creation, with her body being drawn forth from Adam's, they would have formed a two-headed body similar to those of the other creatures and thus asserted close affinities between the natures of Adam and Eve.

The mosaicists also explain visually what theologians strained for centuries to understand: how could a creature as perfect as Adam fail? This motivational problem in the narrative is solved at San Marco by creating an Eve who was less than Adam from the moment of her birth. Using hindsight gained from a later point in the narrative, where Eve desires knowledge and is deceived, the mosaicists emend the story to show her at birth as lacking in knowledge and susceptible to deception; because of her postlapsarian punishment of carnal desire for her husband and childbearing, they create in her prelapsarian state an inherent affinity for the tree associated with carnal knowledge.[22]

The inclusion of a blue Tree of Knowledge at Eve's birth may be unique in the history of art, yet the ideas it reflects are of Augustinian origin, and the motif relates closely to other Italian images primarily of the twelfth and thirteenth centuries. In one of the same passages referred to above, where Augustine identifies the angel-day observers with the Light of the first day and sees them as representing knowledge, he further suggests that Adam's and Eve's souls were made on Day One and stored away until later joined with their bodies in Genesis 2.[23] Nine Umbrian-Roman Creation cycles include this unusual event of the creation of the *souls* of Adam and Eve, an Augustinian scene that precedes the traditional images of Adam's and Eve's bodily creations (Plates 9 and 10 and Fig. 17).[24] In these representations, all hierarchically composed to show the picture's honored right and less-honored left on either side of the central Deity, Adam's and Eve's souls are shown as nude males and females, red and blue respectively, and in most they are surrounded by red and blue mandorlas. In several, the red figure is distinguished from the blue because it emits rays of light. In five examples, God blesses the red being to his right (Adam's soul) and condemns or simply gestures toward the blue soul to his left (Eve's). This tradition, related to that in the San Marco mosaics, similarly attributes binary spiritual qualities of enlightenment and darkness to the first parents from the moment of their creation. Even more important, it aligns their souls with the other events of Day One, specifically, with the creation and fall of the good and bad angels. Four examples, including the earliest from

FIGURE 17.

*Creation of the Souls
of Adam and Eve,*
seventeenth-century
copy of the lost fresco
in St. Paul's, Rome,
c. 700, Rome, Biblio-
teca Vaticana, Cod.
Barb. 4406, fol. 25r.

about 700 (Fig. 17), heighten the opposition between Adam and Eve by
showing Eve's soul turning away from God in a pose that anticipates both
her traditional Expulsion posture and that of the condemned in Last Judgment scenes.[25] All four were monumental, public images, and three were
located in Rome and so could have been of interest to Venice owing to the
city's revival as the New Rome. The fourth, by the Roman school artist
Jacopo Torriti for San Francesco in Assisi (see Plate 9), heightens Eve's
binary opposition to the Virgin Mary, who was herself immaculately conceived. While this latter idea was a matter of controversy in the thirteenth
century, it was championed by prominent Franciscans. Torriti's fresco
showing Eve's defective nature faces Mary at the Annunciation on the opposite wall of this Franciscan church and reminds the viewer of this difference; the sin of the old Eve will be cured by the new.

The San Marco mosaicists seem not to specify that Adam's and Eve's
souls were made on Day One, yet they refer to this binary alignment of
the first couple's souls with the good and bad angels by including the reference to the red and blue angels on Day One and by juxtaposing Eve with
the blue tree at her creation. This theological position on the nature of
Eve's soul was widely held by contemporary theologians, for example by
Thomas Aquinas in his *Summa theologica* of about 1265–72. Like the mosaicists in Venice, he draws on Augustine but also modifies the patriarch's
positions. Aquinas regards Adam as the unitary ancestor of humans,

consisting of both male spirit and female corporeality, and understands Eve's creation to be a separation of that female corporeality from him. Less pessimistic and dualistic than Augustine, Aquinas nonetheless still defines Adam's nature as essentially linked to his rational soul, while Eve's remains linked to the body and procreation.[26] Adam and Eve were not created simultaneously as the other paired animals were because Eve's creation from the rib of the already formed Adam confirms her subordination and inferiority. Females are defective males, passive where males are active, and deficient in intellect. While both are made in the image of God—and here Aquinas qualifies his statement, as did all theologians—the male possesses that image in a superior way, just as there are superior and inferior angels.[27] We see this position of separate and unequal at San Marco, and interestingly, because it is unlikely that Aquinas's views could have been formulated in time to influence the mosaicists in the first cupola, we see the same comparison between male and female humans and the good and bad angels.

Finally, an important gesture overlooked by scholars confirms Eve's carnal nature. For the creations of both Adam and Eve (see Fig. 8 and Plate 7), the Creator forms their bodies with his right hand while holding their wrists in a gesture of restraint with his left.[28] God's left hand on Adam's arm, awkwardly positioned but clearly pointing, gestures upward in the general direction of Adam's head; as Aquinas and many others define his role, "the man is the head of the woman."[29] God's left hand on Eve's arm, by contrast, points down toward her pudendum; we have seen that the word immediately above her is "CARNE[M]" and that her inferior soul is linked to generation. As with Michelangelo's later Eve (Fig. 18), who raises her middle finger toward her own "port of sin," we see a foretelling here of where Eve's destiny will lie. Following the Fall, Adam will rename the woman "Eve," the mother of all living (Gen. 3:20), and her role will be procreation. Once again it is Augustine who underlies the theological perspectives of the San Marco program, for he indicates that God had foreseen from the beginning that *"Eve bore history within her womb."*[30]

This acceptance of the male/spirit–female/body dualism, a denial of Eve's perfection prior to the Fall, explains the Fall. Like the fallen angels, Eve was created good by God, but because of her inferior reason, pride overtakes her; thus weakened, she exercises her free will and sins, falling into darkness. The story as depicted here is not really a developmental one, where we move from initial perfection to imperfection, but essen-

FIGURE 18.

Michelangelo, detail
from *The Fall of Adam
and Eve*, Sistine Chapel
ceiling, 1508–12,
Rome, The Vatican.

tially etiological, for we see why Eve failed.[31] The creations of Adam and
Eve, then, are like those of Light and Darkness, of the firmament and the
earth, of the sun and the moon. All are acts of separation and privation.
Adam's and Eve's bodies will remain opposites—at different sides of compositions, facing each other rather than in parallel—until sin first brings
them closer together (see Figs. 23 and 24) and finally the act of conceiving
the murderous Cain joins them (see Fig. 28).

FIGURE 19.

Introduction of Eve to Adam, detail of the Creation cupola, San Marco, Venice.

CHAPTER FOUR

The First Couple in Paradise

The remainder of the narrative cycle fulfills the implications of Eve's disastrous creation, and her visual signification continues to be "difference." She appears at the picture's left in eight of her twelve scenes at San Marco, her pose a mirrored reversal of the Creator's. In only one episode is she in his active-agent posture, yet that scene represents her worst moment theologically, when she gives the fruit to Adam (see Fig. 20).

The scene following her creation is one of the few in which Eve is central and is therefore a crucial image. God presents Eve to the now alert Adam (Fig. 19), and we are momentarily reassured by her centrality and upright posture. She seems remarkably like God in her pose. But her passive female nature is clear from her stance, with both hands down at her sides, in contrast with those of the active males surrounding her.[1] God propels Eve forward with his right hand on her shoulder but, consistent with the Genesis text, is silent. Adam gestures appropriately with his right hand, for it is he who is given the authority by the *dixitque* formula to name her "Woman" (Gen. 2:23). An ill omen surfaces here, for Adam stands for the first time at the picture's left and faces the opposite way from his pose in the *Naming of the Animals* (see Fig. 12). And visually, Eve is only an object, presented by one male while viewed and named by the other, the very act of her being named demonstrating that, like the animals, she is a creature to be mastered. Ironically, although Eve stands in the center of the composition, a position syntactically communicating dominance, she is powerless. For the rest of the narrative, her role will be marginal in terms of power and control, yet central to the denouement of human history.

The San Marco mosaics repeat many aspects of their model with remarkable veracity and completeness, particularly in the Creation cupola. Of the thirty-four relevant scenes included in the Cotton Genesis, this cupola omits only four. Surprisingly, we find among the few omissions God's admonition to Adam and Eve regarding the Tree of Knowledge, a scene that in the manuscript almost certainly immediately followed Eve's introduction to Adam. Weitzmann and Kessler reconstruct a single miniature with these two scenes, the admonition at the picture's right, followed by Eve conversing with the Serpent (Eve shown first and the Serpent last, at the picture's left). While the Vulgate text differs—for there God warns *only* Adam regarding the Tree, just after introducing him to Paradise, and prior to Eve's creation—most medieval accounts of the Fall, verbal and visual, logically emend the story to make both present; many images, including the fifth-century Cotton Genesis, comply.[2]

At San Marco, however, the mosaicists have deliberately altered this tradition. We saw already that the admonition was restored to its original narrative location at *Adam's Introduction into Paradise* (see Fig. 10); the result of this is to enable the mosaicists to omit it here. The change from the model allows the viewer to account for Eve's greater weakness toward the Serpent, for she can know of the prohibition only secondhand from Adam.

The Serpent and the Blue Tree of Knowledge

The Serpent plays an important role in the *Temptation of Eve* (Plate 11), and trees are once again significant. The mosaicists extensively rearranged the Cotton Genesis composition, allotting the privileged first position, most closely associated with the Creator, to the upright Serpent. This accords well with the Vulgate text, for the Serpent here is twice given the speaking formula also associated with God, the *dixit* cue (Gen. 3:1 and

3 :4). Eve does not initiate conversation with the Serpent but only answers when spoken to ("cui respondit mulier," Gen. 3 : 2); thus her secondary position and reversed, mirror-image posture with right hand raised in speech are appropriate.[3] The mosaicists' repositioning also clarifies the hierarchy of authority. Further, the Serpent inhabits a blue tree that reveals his unenlightened and fallen nature and identifies him as the agent of Lucifer, the leader of the fallen angels who came into being when Light and Darkness were separated.[4] Weitzmann and Kessler suggest that the anomalous figure of Adam standing with his back to Eve is a vestige of the episode of God's admonition, now missing from the Cotton Genesis, but that he originally almost certainly came first in the frame, before Eve and the Serpent.[5] However, Adam's inclusion by the thirteenth-century mosaicists is not incidental, as these scholars imply; rather, it clarifies his role in the Fall.

Like Eve, the Serpent helps to explain Adam's fall from perfection, for he, too, functions as an intermediary in a chain of deception descending from Lucifer to Adam. The question of Eve's susceptibility to the Serpent's speech was thus an important one, and in this scene the compositional alterations from the Cotton Genesis manuscript make it more plausible. Moving the Serpent to the Creator's position heightens his authority in the image, and his placement in the blue tree, first seen next to Eve at her creation, suggests their immediate likeness. The idea of a natural affinity between the Woman and the Serpent—later to be abolished by a punitive Deity when he declares enmity between them—was affirmed by theologians such as Peter Comestor and his fifteenth-century English translator, William Caxton. Comestor explains the Serpent's addressing of Eve both by Eve's spiritual weakness and their physical affinity. First he writes that the Woman is "minus providam et certam, in vitium flecti aggressus est," which Caxton translates as "not so prudent and more prone to slide and bow,"[6] and then he suggests a further similarity between the Serpent and Eve that became enormously popular in medieval and renaissance art, although it was not used at San Marco. According to Comestor, the Serpent had the head of a female; thus Eve was more likely to listen to and trust this creature. At San Marco, this same affinity between the Woman and the Serpent is expressed differently, through the proximity of both to the blue tree at important moments in the narrative; the blue tree further connects both to the final link in the chain of disobedience, the proud Lucifer.[7]

It is traditional that the Serpent's tree is the Tree of Knowledge of

FIGURE 20.

Eve Plucking the Fruit and Tempting Adam, detail of the Creation cupola, San Marco, Venice.

Good and Evil. Here its blue color reveals the tree's inherently closer kinship with evil and the fallen angels than with good. But puzzlingly, the trees against which Eve's body is silhouetted are specifically identifiable as fig trees, for in the following scene she will pluck fruit not from the blue tree but from a fig tree (Fig. 20); only later in the narrative does the blue tree reappear adjacent to the Tree of Life (see Fig. 24).[8] None of these trees, of course, corresponds botanically to the Tree of Knowledge depicted earlier in Adam's introduction to Paradise and his admonition (see Fig. 10), but all must be associated with Eve and the Serpent, with disobedience and evil. This ambiguity regarding the identity of the Tree could deny the exegetical position that the fruit of the Tree of Knowledge was actually poisonous and favor an alternative theory that the Tree itself was harmless but the act of disobedience brought death.[9] Evil is subtle and difficult for even a knowledgeable soul to recognize. The blueness of the tree emphasizes that privation of knowledge leads to disobedience; the fig remains innocent.

Adam is included in the scene of Eve's temptation but blatantly turns his back on both her and the Serpent, a kind of inside-out version of the extremely common and even formulaic scene in medieval art of Adam and Eve standing symmetrically to either side of the Serpent coiled around the Tree of Knowledge (see Plate 8). Unlike the Vulgate, the Hebrew text of Genesis and accounts such as Josephus's have the Serpent addressing Adam as well as Eve,[10] but here the mosaics assert that Adam is ignorant of any such encounter or, if he hears it, turns away. The mosaicists, by including an uninterested Adam rather than simply omitting him, powerfully reinforce his uninvolvement. Simultaneously, we understand the Serpent's logic in approaching Eve. Well established as the spiritually susceptible one, Eve will sin; her disobedience will ensnare the more godlike Adam.

The *titulus* above the *Temptation of Eve*, not an abbreviated version of the Vulgate text but, for the first time, an invented one, also exonerates Adam from guilt, laying the blame squarely on the Serpent and Eve. Astonishingly didactic and blunt, it chronicles the first human—and female—action carried out without the guiding presence of the Creator: "HIC SERPENS LOQVITVR EVE ET DECIPIT EAM." It actually summarizes what *will* happen, for even before Eve plucks the fruit, eats (as she does in the fourth of the four Cotton Genesis miniatures omitted in the cupola), and gives it to Adam, we are informed that "Here the Serpent speaks to Eve and deceives her." The subtext is that Adam, present visually although uninvolved, and blatantly omitted from the text, is not deceived.[11] Oddly, he is gesturing with his right hand, which usually indicates speech, but does not seem to say anything. Adam actually speaks (*dixit* and *ait*) only three times in Genesis and in addition names (*appellavitque*) the animals, and all four occurrences appear here at San Marco with the appropriate gesture in the correct scene. But no speech exists to fit this speaking gesture.[12] The pose instead reminds the viewer at this crucial narrative juncture of Adam's essential similarity to the active-agent Creator. It also emphasizes by contrast Eve's backwardness and intensifies the soon-to-be-seen difference of Adam's altered posture during and after his sin.[13]

The inscriptions for the final nine scenes in the cupola, beginning here with the *Temptation of Eve*, are all invented, nonbiblical texts, and all begin with "HIC" ("Here"). This change comes at the same point in the account (Gen. 3:1) where the mood of the written narrative changes, by becoming historical after the ahistorical opening chapters. As Mieke Bal has noted in her studies of Genesis, the Serpent at this moment introduces the possibility of action into the story.[14] The text also substitutes the present-tense verb *loquitur* for the perfect-tense *dixit*, the word used in the Vulgate text. Unlike the visual language, which enhances the godlike authority of the Serpent by its pose and position within the composition, the *titulus* avoids the connotations of authority and finality offered by *dixit;* simultaneously, however, it brings the action into the world of the viewer's here and now.

Adam Sins

Adam's loss of his godlike perfection manifests visually through his changed posture and compositional placement in the scenes following Eve's Fall. We see this first in *Eve Plucking the Fruit and Tempting Adam* (see Fig. 20), a two-part scene that completes this multiepisodic version of the Fall. It opens with the Tree of Knowledge in the Deity's usual position, followed by a still retrograde Eve plucking a fig from it. A second scene follows in the same frame that places Eve first, before the fig, and turned toward Adam. About to sin, he stands to the picture's left and is retrograde, a simile for Eve in three of her four previous appearances. Eve, too, appears transformed, for she stands erect, right hand raised, on the privileged side at the picture's right of the scene, and facing Adam. This remarkable scene is the only mosaic in the entire cycle where Eve stands in the active-agent pose of the Creator.[15] The visual syntax asserts Eve's authoritative-ness and demonstrates her resemblance to her Creator, but ironically her pose expresses her sin rather than positive traits. She acts out of evil pride—like the fallen angels, she aspires to be like the Creator—and her ambition results in the Fall. She has already eaten, her eyes are open fully, and she *is* briefly like God, "knowing good and evil" (Gen. 3:5), just as the Serpent has promised her.[16] Although God later mentions only Adam ("Behold, Adam is become as one of us, knowing good and evil"; Gen. 3:22), the mosaicists remind us that Eve, too, attained this remarkable state of being.

But while the mosaic illustrates the truth of the Serpent's prediction, it emphasizes a key distinction from the Creator's pose. Eve stands in profile. She will appear in profile in four more of her seven remaining appearances (see Figs. 24–26 and Plate 2), conforming with the Byzantine convention of showing evil beings in profile so as to avoid the dangers of eye contact with the viewer.[17] Eve may have used her godlike authority to tempt Adam, but at this moment the mosaicists wish to prevent her interaction with us.

PLATE 1.

Creation cupola,
thirteenth century,
atrium of San Marco,
Venice.

ETE VA HICEXPELLITEOSDEPARADISO:HICINCIPIUTLABORARE:EXPELLAVIT

CHERVBIN CRISTIELA

PLATE 2.

The Expulsion and the
Labors of Adam and Eve,
detail of the Creation
cupola, San Marco,
Venice.

PLATE 4.

Creation of the Heavenly Bodies, detail of the Creation cupola, San Marco, Venice.

PLATE 5.

Blessing of the Birds and Marine Creatures, detail of the Creation cupola, San Marco, Venice.

PLATE 7.

Creation of Eve, detail
of the Creation cupola,
San Marco, Venice.

PLATE 9.

Jacopo Torriti, *Creation of the Souls of Adam and Eve*, c. 1290, Upper Church of San Francesco, Assisi.

Creation of the Souls of Adam and Eve, Creation of Adam, and *Creation of Eve* (with story of Joseph below), Tuscan artists, c. 1270–90, baptistry of San Giovanni, Florence.

PLATE II.

Temptation of Eve,
detail of the Creation
cupola, San Marco,
Venice.

PLATE 12.

God in the Act of Creation with His Compass, Holkham Bible Picture Book, English, early fourteenth century, London, British Library, Ms. Add. 47682, fol. 2r.

Jewish and Christian exegetes repeatedly addressed the question of why Adam sinned. Adam was not deficient from the moment of his creation, nor was he deprived of enlightenment and driven by a proud desire to be "like" his Creator. Adam's sin was explained differently. According to one popular tradition, it was the result of his love for Eve and his loyal desire to remain with her even after her error.[18] The mosaicists here align themselves with two other traditions, first, that Eve seduced Adam with words, and second, that Adam acted out of lust.[19] Eve uses both her hands in this important scene. Her right hand is raised, not because she just gave the fruit to Adam, but—as seen consistently in the visual syntax of these mosaics—to indicate speech. Oddly, at this point of high drama in the story, the Vulgate does not accord a speaking role to Eve. Speech, like the active-agent posture that represents it in the mosaics, is a form of validation for characters in the Old Testament, a privilege rarely accorded to either Adam or Eve. Eve speaks four times, once each in reply to the Serpent and God in Eden, and once each in her postlapsarian role of procreator and name-giver at the births of Cain and Seth, scenes omitted at San Marco, although present in the Cotton Genesis. She never, however, earns the *dixit* or *ait* formulas associated with the Creator and Adam.[20] The mosaicists here, by raising Eve's right hand and placing her in a posture of authority, convey that she spoke to Adam to beguile him, an interpretation consistent with God's later punishment of Adam, condemning him "because thou hast hearkened to the voice of thy wife" (Gen. 3:17).

But the image hints at a second explanation for Adam's sin. Eve's left hand gestures downward toward Adam's pudendum, as does the gaze of her profiled head, a head posture not seen in adjacent depictions of her. Similar to God's pointing at Eve's pudendum during her forming, Eve's glance and gesture anticipate the roles that lust and Adam's corporeal nature will now play in human history. And her eyes here have opened to the shame of their nakedness while Adam's eyes have not; she sees and knows what Adam does not.

After the Fall

In *Adam and Eve Covering Their Nakedness* (Fig. 21), Adam appears first in the scene, but no longer in the *imago dei*. A sinner, his likeness to God is syntactically negated by his backward posture; he reaches into the fig tree for leaves, exactly echoing the figure of Eve plucking the fig in the previous

FIGURE 21.

Adam and Eve Covering Their Nakedness, detail of the Creation cupola, San Marco, Venice.

scene. Eve's posture is contorted; her head turns back toward Adam, her torso twists toward the succeeding scene, and one leg crosses over the other. This leg posture, common for Eve figures in medieval and renaissance art, is a visual simile for the Serpent winding around the Tree of Knowledge. It signifies the carnal/sexual nature of the sin inside her and will reappear in the figure of Potiphar's wife, the seductress in the Joseph story (Fig. 22). When God comes looking for Eve and Adam in the following scene, *Adam and Eve Hiding from God* (Fig. 23), her legs again overlap—unlike those of any other standing figure in the cupola—and her serpentine arms crisscross her twisted torso. Adam, also agitated, runs from the dignified and still static Creator. Having acquired divine knowledge, they are at this moment *most like* God, yet their twisted and bent postures here and in the successive scenes appear most ungodlike and reveal the enormity of their sin.[21] Adam's completely altered posture, aligned now with Eve's instead of God's, reveals immediately his state of sin. God calls

to Adam, his right hand raised in speech; Adam's reply comes similarly via his right hand. Insulting the Deity, the deceptive Eve, hiding but not speaking, raises her left hand toward him.

According to the Vulgate text, the *Denial of Guilt* (Fig. 24) immediately follows the speeches of God and Adam in the previous scene; however, the mosaicists deny the scene absolute proximity by seating God on an elaborate throne and changing the setting to the very center of Eden, where the Trees of Life and Knowledge grow. Although Adam and Eve are both still retrograde, Adam stands closer to the Tree of Life and God, suggesting once again that he is the more redeemable of the two first parents. The Tree of Knowledge reappears as a slim, erect blue tree, associated with the Serpent, Eve, and Darkness, and grows appropriately next to the Tree of Life, behind the throne of God, where it is protected from further encroachment by the first couple. The Serpent is omitted, although it traditionally appears in images of this scene, and art historians have remarked

FIGURE 22.

Potiphar Making Joseph Overseer, detail of the second Joseph cupola, San Marco, Venice.

FIGURE 23.

Adam and Eve Hiding from God, detail of the Creation cupola, San Marco, Venice.

its absence here. However, the San Marco mosaicists in this matter ally themselves with the Vulgate tradition, as reiterated and explained by writers like Comestor, rather than with some popular treatments of the narrative from the later Middle Ages that added an episode of God's interrogating the Serpent. Comestor's well-known view held that the Serpent was not questioned because he was only the agent of Lucifer, not Lucifer himself; we recall that the Serpent was present at God's blessing above (see Plate 5).[22]

The Vulgate text, beginning with the episode of Adam and Eve hiding, consists entirely of conversations, and the mosaicists represent each of these by appropriately postured figures in three successive images. The complexity of these closely spaced episodes warrants a careful look at the correspondence of words and images. In *Adam and Eve Hiding* (Fig. 23), God's right hand signals his one speech to Adam, asking where he is (*dixit*, Gen. 3:9b), while Adam's right hand indicates his answer (*ait*, 3:10). Eve

does not speak, but raises her left hand. In the *Denial of Guilt* (Fig. 24), all three actors gesture with right hands, and these gestures denote, respectively, God's asking Adam if he has eaten of the Tree (*dixit*, 3:11), Adam's reply that the woman gave him the fruit (*dixit*, 3:12), God's questioning of Eve (*dixit*, 3:13a, returning us to the Creator figure a second time), and finally Eve's reply that the Serpent deceived her (*respondit*, 3:13b). God immediately speaks to punish the wrongdoers in the *Punishment of the Serpent, Eve, and Adam* (Fig. 25). With raised right hand, he first curses the Serpent (*ait*, 3:14–15), then punishes Eve (*dixit*, 3:16), and finally Adam (*dixit*, 3:17–19).

Thus, in the Denial, God asks only Adam and Eve, not the Serpent, about what they have done, and both answer, though Adam still uses the godlike *dixit* and Eve the more passive *respondit*. Eve in the Vulgate does reply that the Serpent tempted her, but here the Latin text above the mosaic, again part of an invented text not derived from the Vulgate, ignores

FIGURE 24.

Denial of Guilt, detail of the Creation cupola, San Marco, Venice.

FIGURE 25.

Punishment of the Serpent, Eve, and Adam, detail of the Creation cupola, San Marco, Venice.

the Serpent's role in her disobedience: "HIC DOMINVS INCREPAT ADAM IPSE MONSTRAT VXOREM FVISSE CAVSAM" ("Here the Lord rebukes Adam who himself shows that his wife was the cause"). In this version of the famous "passing the buck" scene, altered from the Cotton Genesis model by omitting the guilty Serpent, Adam speaks and points to Eve, laying the blame squarely on her.[23] Only her speech gesture—and, if viewers remembered, the corresponding Vulgate text—would attribute guilt to the Serpent, for visually Eve accepts her responsibility by not pointing elsewhere.[24] Her profiled face, contrasting with God's and Adam's, implies her guilt, and of course the mosaicists had prepared the viewers for her culpability since her creation. God's enthronement like a presiding judge, another detail altered from the fifth-century model, confirms the gravity of the moment and emphasizes the theme of accusation, trial, and judgment. His static, stately position contrasts with the submissively bent and agitated poses of Adam and Eve, visually reassuring us of his eternal divinity even at this moment, when in the J text he appears less than omnipotent.[25] An eschatological passage from the *Vita Adae et Evae* may have provided a source for the mosaicists, for there, as soon as Adam eats, Eve relates:

> And in the same hour, we heard the archangel Michael sounding his trumpet, calling the angels, saying, "Thus says the Lord, 'Come with me into Paradise and hear the sentence which I pronounce on Adam.'" And as we heard the archangel sounding the trumpet, we said, "Behold, God is coming into Paradise to judge us." . . . And the throne of God was made ready where the tree of life was.[26]

The specification of locale—the middle of the Garden where both the Tree of Life and the Tree of Knowledge are—further corresponds with the San Marco mosaic.

The Serpent, out of its tree with head lowered, reappears only in the *Punishment of the Serpent, Eve, and Adam* (Fig. 25), where it appears first in the scene, for God addresses it immediately following Eve's explanation in the previous episode. In a frontal, symmetrical composition reminiscent of a Last Judgment,[27] the centrally enthroned God gestures with his right hand, with Adam kneeling to his right and Eve to his left. As in the preceding scene, God's gesture represents a series of speeches, hierarchically addressed first to the lowly Serpent, then to Eve, and finally to Adam. But although both the text and the composition are hierarchically composed, the two, oddly, do not absolutely correspond. The lowliest of the characters, the Serpent more logically would be placed at the picture's left, lower than Eve. However, its unusual position—even farther to the picture's right than Adam himself—momentarily maintains the fast pace of the narrative, where the Serpent is the object of God's first curse, and its distance from Eve reflects the enmity God puts between the woman and the Serpent; at least its lowered head demonstrates its inferiority. Adam and Eve, now both static and in profile, remain appropriately displayed, Adam on the more honored and Eve on the more sinister side. The Latin text confirms that the artists knew the Serpent was cursed first, for it states, "HIC DOMINVS MALEDICIT SERPENTI CVM ADAM ET EVA ANTE SE EXISTEN-TIBVS" (Here the Lord curses the Serpent with Adam and Eve appearing before him).

In the following, very rarely depicted scene, God dresses Adam and Eve (Fig. 26), and the rigid, symmetrical composition retains the stern mood

FIGURE 26.

*God Dressing Adam and
Eve*, detail of the Cre-
ation cupola, San
Marco, Venice.

of judgment established in the previous two episodes. God helps the still-profiled Eve with her garment as the already clothed Adam looks on, and the episode possibly refers to the early Christian notion that when God clothed Adam and Eve, they received their newly mortal corporeality.[28] Although in the next scene her clothing is identical to Adam's and easily covers her legs, here it exposes them. Bared legs were a sign of sexuality, and possibly the newly knowledgeable Adam's down-tilted head indicates his corporeal interest in Eve's naked limbs.[29]

The *Expulsion* and the *Labors of Adam and Eve* (see Plate 2) occupy the final frame of the lowest register of the cupola. The two episodes move easily from the viewer's left to right and reestablish the movement of the narrative after the more static preceding images. The first half of the frame is crowded, including initially the Tree of Life with a cross in its branches, two phoenixes, and a flaming sword below, followed by the erect figure of the Creator with two hands on Adam's shoulder pushing him and Eve out the portal of Paradise. As in the scene of Eve's creation, the Tree of Life is a type for the Cross of Christ, for the Crucifixion will be the cure for the sin that led to Expulsion. As noted above, the reference to the wood of the Cross is probably also inspired by San Marco's own relic of the True Cross in its Treasury. The phoenixes represent the resurrected Christ and here are red, the color at San Marco associated with enlightenment and the good angels, who did not fall. They are, indeed, enlightened, for according to Jewish legend, Eve offered to share the forbidden fruit with all the animals, but only the phoenixes refused and so were allowed to stay in Paradise.[30]

The popular *Vita Adae et Evae* may again be a source for the mosaicists, in this case for a reordering of elements from the Cotton Genesis. Weitzmann and Kessler reconstruct the Cotton Genesis manuscript with a scene following the *Expulsion* and prior to the *Labors of Adam and Eve* of a cherub (or cherubim) outside Eden guarding the way back to the Tree of Life with a flaming sword, as described in Genesis 3:23–24.[31] San Marco, on the other hand, includes the flaming sword first in the scene below the Tree of Life and links the Tree to the Crucifixion and Resurrection, all in accordance with the text of the *Vita*. There, before Adam is expelled from Eden, the Lord warns him:

> "You shall not now take from it [the Tree of Life]; for it was appointed to the cherubim and the flaming sword which turns to guard it because of you, that you might not taste of it and be immortal forever. . . . [But] if you guard yourself from all evil, preferring death to it, at the time of the resurrection I will raise you again, and then there shall be given to you from the tree of life, and you shall be immortal forever."[32]

Eve and Adam stand erect in the *Expulsion* and appear more dignified than in previous scenes, but both are in profile and make large gestures with their prominent left hands toward their new, extraparadisal environment. Their right hands hold the tools of their mundane trades, a mattock for Adam and a spindle and distaff for Eve. Eve looks back eagerly at Adam, showing him the world with which the Middle Ages associated her, the earthly realm. Her eagerness and gesture ironically echo those of the Creator in the *Introduction of Adam into Paradise* (see Figs. 10 and 11), the scene immediately above this one. In that scene God similarly turns and looks back toward Adam as he pulls him into the Eden from which he now expels the pair.

Eve's and Adam's bodies, covered by matching animal skins, stand closer together than in any other scene and appear identical. While they began their relationship as opposites, Eve representing the difference that heightened Adam's perfection, their shared sin finally unites them. Once again the viewer is reminded of apocalyptic imagery, specifically Judgment scenes, with damned souls pushed into the jaws of Hell. Here, though, God himself propels them toward the picture's lower left, the traditional location of Hell in Judgment images.[33] The cherubim, who in the Genesis text guard the way back to the Tree of Life, appear in the pendentives below the cupola, defending the cupola itself from violation by the descendants of Adam and Eve, depicted in the mosaics of the adjacent lunettes and barrel vault; one is located immediately below the portal itself (see Fig. 11). They also guard the Tree and the Garden from us, the viewers standing in the earthly realm below.

CHAPTER FIVE

The Labors of Adam and Eve

The Newly Mortal Adam and Eve

The final scene in the dome begins the saga of the earthly tale of Adam and Eve (see Plate 2). We find Eve enthroned with spindle and distaff while Adam toils to till the earth with his mattock, both their bodies positioned below the horizon. On the one hand, as in the scene where she tempts Adam (see Fig. 20), Eve seems to have attained her goal of being like God: here she is the side issue neither visually nor theologically, but the central, frontal figure. Seated on a golden throne, elsewhere in the cycle an attribute only of the Deity, she appears regal, holding her distaff like a scepter and staring at Adam while he looks down at the ground. Yet the treatment of her body suggests a different message. Eve's physique is transformed in comparison to its depiction in the adjacent scene of the Expulsion; it has become expressly female and remarkably voluptuous. Her dress has also changed, for a light blue fillet now ornaments her hair and a blue belt gathers her garment below her breasts. Her body is again twisted, with her torso facing Paradise and her head turned toward Adam and the earthly environment. The landscape is simple, with few plants and a pair of sheep, but this simplicity is deceptive, for the mosaic is complex in meaning. In the context of the preceding scenes, we can begin to understand the conflicting roles of the newly mortal Adam and Eve.

Interpreters of the Genesis text had etiological goals, and we have seen that the unknown planner of the San Marco mosaics certainly did as well. The cupola functions didactically as a mirror—and its circularity is like that of the convex mirrors in use at this time—into which viewers gaze and find explanations for why we are as we are.[1] This purpose becomes particularly relevant in these last scenes because Adam and Eve appear for the first time outside Eden, in our own human environment: they have become Everyman and Everywoman; their roles, our roles. Why must we work? Why must women be submissive to their husbands and bring forth their children in sorrow? Why do we die? Thus, in a generic way, Adam represents all men who labor physically to survive, his agricultural work aligning him with one of the basic tasks of human existence. Figures of men plowing and hoeing, enduring Adam's curse, appear in countless cycles depicting the Labors of the Months in manuscripts and on church facades—including the west portals of San Marco. These ubiquitous cycles further confirm the universality and timelessness of Adam's human tasks. Similarly, Eve holds the tools of spinning, a labor long associated with women and the domestic household in Western civilization.[2] According to late-thirteenth-century matrimonial law in Venice, on the eighth day of marriage—parallel to the first day of post-Edenic existence for Eve—women were presented with distaffs and spindles.[3] Yet at San Marco, we are once again struck by difference. No dutiful model of behavior, Eve sits in a pose that emphasizes her inactivity. Idle and enthroned, her hair uncovered, she represents luxurious aspects of female nature, not wifely industriousness. The post-Edenic Eve and Adam thus continue the medieval binary system of difference.

The standard explanation for Eve's enthroned posture and her attributes here is that she functions as an antitype for the Virgin Mary. This Western typological formulation, popular in the twelfth and thirteenth centuries, is encapsulated in the well-known Eva/Ave formula of reversal.[4] Such comparison of the woman who closes the door to Paradise with the woman who reopens it *is* present in this complex figure, as confirmed by the theme's popularity in roughly contemporary mosaics in Italy, for example, at Monreale, Torcello, Murano, and even in the twelfth-century mosaics in the Cappella Zen of San Marco itself.[5] The allusion to Mary also complements the typological references from the Old Adam to the New in the *Creation of Eve* and the *Expulsion*, for the Old Eve will similarly yield to the New.

The incident in Mary's life suggested by her antitype's distaff and her childless enthronement is the Annunciation, an event of particular interest in Venice. Tradition held that the city was founded in 421 on March 25, the day of the Feast of the Annunciation; because of this, Mary was the chief patron saint of the Republic of Venice.[6] According to the *Protevangelium of James*, Mary was spinning wool for the temple cloth when Gabriel came to her, an episode frequently depicted in medieval art, particularly in Byzantine Annunciations, and thus familiar to Venetian audiences.[7] Certain works in the West could also have influenced the artists at San Marco, particularly with their interest in reassociating themselves with Early Christian Rome. For example, Mary in the fifth-century *Annunciation* at Santa Maria Maggiore in Rome sits similarly enthroned, with distaff and diadem (Fig. 27).[8] But Eve remains an antitype, not a type, for Mary, for the very qualities the mosaicists stress—her susceptibility to Lucifer via the Serpent's deceptive speech, her pride leading to disobedience, her carnal desire for her husband resulting in the conception of Cain—directly oppose those of Mary, who listens to the archangel Gabriel, humbly obeys God, and miraculously conceives Christ by the Word. Where Mary is the rose, Eve is the thorn, the plant God makes to grow in Adam's earthly garden. We must not forget, however, that Eve's role is central in the drama. As in her relationship to Adam, Eve's difference helps to clarify Mary's being. For all her otherness, Eve nonetheless projects us forward in human history to the story of Redemption.

The Punishments

Perhaps the best way to further our explanation for this particular scene of the Labors is to consider the nature of God's punishments for Adam and Eve's disobedience. The operative notion, popular in contemporary Hell scenes as well, is that all things are ironically reversed in the end: former

pleasures become eternal tortures, and punishments fit the crime. Thus
Adam's and Eve's postlapsarian punishments yield a clearer understanding
of their prelapsarian states. For example, the Genesis text never specifies
Adam's prelapsarian immortality, yet his punishment of returning to dust
implies that he had been immortal.[9] Similarly for Eve, implications regarding her character prior to the Expulsion are absent from the Genesis text
until the meting out of punishments retroactively establishes them. In a
reversal of temporal cause and effect, the nature of their punishments *creates* their prelapsarian selves and simultaneously explains what prompted
them to sin. Further, certain qualities directly opposed to those understood in the Middle Ages as natural for man, woman, or serpent were imputed to their Edenic natures, suggesting that human nature in our earthly
lives results from God's punishments for the Fall.

In the case of the Serpent, for example, our greatest knowledge concerning its original nature comes from the conditions of its punishment. God's curse condemns it to move on its belly and eat dust, and creates enmity between the Serpent and the Woman and between its issue and her issue (Gen. 3:14–15), who will crush the Serpent's head; writers like Josephus add logically that the Serpent lost its power of speech at this moment.[10] We infer from these corrections that in its prelapsarian state it traveled erect, spoke, and had a natural affinity for the Woman, soon to be renamed Eve. All these qualities help establish motivations within the narrative, making it more logical that Eve would be susceptible to this creature that women now "naturally" fear.

Adam's two punishments similarly highlight his prelapsarian qualities. The once-powerful and godlike Adam is condemned to toil to produce his bread, to work the cursed earth, which will willingly yield only thistles and thorns. Thus he has traded in his once-lush and productive environment, where he had merely "to dress it, and to keep it" (Gen. 2:15), for a hostile milieu requiring hard labor. His second punishment is that he must die, returning to that same earth he now works. In fact, the Creator expels Adam from Paradise specifically so that he will not eat of the Tree of Life and "live for ever" (Gen. 3:22). Mortality is the human condition, now that Adam is no longer godlike. The loss of these divine qualities is shown visually by his bent, profiled body, dressed in the skin of mortality and now located at the picture's lower left corner, far from his former location at the picture's right. Adam, who began the tale more perfect than Eve, has fallen farther than she. His prelapsarian reason, which established his dominion over the animals, is now tainted; his low posture demonstrates his affinity with the beasts, and the two animals that graze above him in the mosaic are in a syntactically superior location. Thomas of Cîteaux reports that the postlapsarian Adam became like a quadruped, with his stomach toward the ground, and John of Salisbury explains, "Rationalis creatura *brutescit. Sic imago Creatori deformatur in bestiam*" ("The rational creature loses reason. Thus the image of the Creator is deformed into a beast").[11] As is normal in the Middle Ages, metaphysical ideas are demonstrated physically, as the outside reflects the inside. And finally, the mosaicists show a sexual reversal—a feminization—of Adam. *His* leg is bared, revealed to Eve's desirous gaze. In an inversion of the divine hierarchy, he appears subject to her.

Eve's punishments, as listed in the Vulgate text, are significantly more severe than Adam's and reveal much about the qualities implicitly associated with her while in Paradise and with women in general. Although the Vulgate text does not explicitly state so, she obviously shares both of Adam's punishments: she, too, suffers the loss of Paradise and must work and live in the hostile earthly environment; and she, too, loses her immortality, as her formerly naked body is now dressed. But Eve must bear additional burdens because of her greater culpability.[12] First, she will have greatly increased pain in childbirth. Augustine, centuries earlier, interpreted this to mean that procreation, like Adam's keeping of the Garden, was already part of the first couple's existence in Paradise, but now would become unpleasant for Eve.[13] An act shared by both sexes—procreation—is identified only with Eve once it becomes a punishment, reaffirming her carnal nature. For her second punishment, the Creator himself condemns her to sin, for she will desire her husband, a state apparently absent from Eve in Paradise but generally attributed to her nonetheless. Jerome altered the sense of this punishment in his Vulgate translation by eliminating this reference to sexual desire and elaborating instead on the idea that Eve would be submissive to Adam, but—perhaps because both the Greek text and imagery of the Cotton Genesis retained the original Hebrew meaning and because Augustine and other early exegetes discussed the text in an Old Latin (non-Vulgate) version—the San Marco mosaics retain this punishment of desire from the original Hebrew text.[14] Thus Eve's postlapsarian nature is condemned by God himself to be ruled by her body and sexuality. Her third punishment, that her husband shall rule over her, certainly responds to Eve's prideful disobedience of God's injunction and reflects the generally held medieval suspicion that women tend toward insubordination. It further implies that even in Eden Eve had some unnamed power over Adam, perhaps her verbal facility or her seductiveness, yet ironically, it also clearly recalls Adam's sin of listening to his wife rather than to his God; in a sense, then, that she shall be submissive to him is his punishment, too. These arguments indulge in the circular reasoning of the retrospective fallacy, where later effects condition the earlier causes and contemporary assumptions legitimate how the past is to be understood.

What aspects of Eve's punishments does the visual language of the mosaicists emphasize? Eve's punishments are more complex than her spouse's and actually occupy not only the *Labors* but also the first two scenes below the cupola in the east lunette (Fig. 28). The final appearance of Eve and

Adam is in the *Birth of Abel*, to our right, a traditionally handled scene that alludes to pain by showing childbirth, although it does not depict discomfort in any specific way. Her second curse, that her desire shall be for her husband, is certainly depicted in the next to last scene of their story, the *Conception of Cain*. Located in the lunette below and immediately to the right of the *Labors* on the bottommost register of the cupola, it continues the spiraling movement of the narrative, its inferior location symbolic of its yet lower spiritual content. This highly unusual scene shows Eve and Adam in bed asleep, the evil of their act and its unfortunate issue implied by their sinister gestures: Adam's left hand caresses Eve's breast, as he shares her curse of desire, and Eve's left hand touches Adam's genitals. The child Eve will bear will himself prove bestial in nature and cause the first human death, a murder.

FIGURE 28.

Conception of Cain and *Birth of Abel*, in east lunette, below the Creation cupola, detail, San Marco, Venice.

Eve and the Power of Women

Eve's third punishment, submissiveness, is God's antidote for Eve's pride and her guileful mastery of Adam. It overtly establishes hierarchy and power as themes in the narrative, and should conventionally be a major concern in the *Labors of Adam and Eve*. Yet this image of Eve is ironic. While we see a reversal of the once-exalted Adam to field laborer, Eve, as we have seen, does not appear humbled at all. Rather, she possesses even more intensely her prelapsarian faults of pride, disobedience, and concupiscence, thus reflecting medieval ideas about real, contemporary women. The one Edenic quality that is reversed is her most fundamental, her inferiority. Not at all submissive or marginal relative to Adam, Eve here occupies the position of power, enthroned and more central, while Adam himself is marginalized—even feminized—by his bent posture, revealing garment, and placement at the picture's left. Eve retains her priority in the following scene of Cain's conception (Fig. 28), where she lies to the picture's right and overlaps Adam's body rather than vice versa. Far from being tamed into submissiveness, she remains dangerous to Adam.

The San Marco *Labors* constitutes an early visual example of the medieval misogynistic "Power of Women" tradition, depicting a topsy-turvy world that exalts Eve as a kind of Queen of Misrule while ridiculing the toiling Adam.[15] The true reversal here is of the divinely ordained hierarchy between man and woman—the "natural" order—and its causes are the very qualities associated with Eve while still in Eden, especially her pride and her carnal nature. The reason for showing the reversal, however, is that it clarifies the real social structure.[16] While there is humor in this ironic image of "Queen" Eve and "peasant" Adam, we are warned not to forget that the mundane world is full of sinful women with powers not to be underestimated. Even Adam, made in the image of the Lord, has fallen to woman's wiles; could the thirteenth-century male viewer expect to fare better? Of course, what the thirteenth-century female viewer, with her inherently defective nature, was to think about the possibility of her own salvation remains unclear.

That Eve still suffers from pride, and in fact personifies that vice, is evinced in several ways in the *Labors*. For example, she is a "proud pauper" in contrast with her hardworking, common laborer husband. Like a mock queen, she sits idly enthroned with her "scepter," proudly dressed in finery, but seated in a barren field. This image resonates strongly with other near contemporary works of art, both earlier and later. The Devil-Serpent in the twelfth-century mystery play *Jeu d'Adam* promises Eve "that thou be queen of the world . . . And be the mistress of them all," but after her Fall, the Lord reprimands her, "Erstwhile thou heldest sovereignty. . . . How quickly hast thou lost thy crown!" [17] Unlike that Eve, the San Marco Eve proudly resists relinquishing her crown. A fifteenth-century Flemish illustration of the *Labors* in the *Speculum humanae salvationis* (Fig. 29), an early-fourteenth-century text that credits the Fall to Eve's vice of pride, similarly juxtaposes a laboring Adam in common garb with an Eve dressed in finery, holding spindle and distaff. The text admonishes, "and he who wishes to be a laborer in the fields, ought not to dress in silk." [18] The personifications of Pride found at the base of the popular Trees of Vices (see, e.g., Figs. 15 and 16) are depicted as enthroned females with crowns and scepters, placed in opposition to plainly adorned Humility. [19] An English example from the Psalter of Robert de Lisle (Fig. 30), illuminated about 1310, demonstrates the pervasiveness of this theme in late medieval Europe. Produced only shortly after the completion of the San Marco mosaics, it shows Eve reaching for the fruit from the mouth of the Serpent entwined in the Tree and simultaneously handing another fruit to Adam. Below the figures of Adam and Eve at the base of the Tree, a Latin text records that Pride is the root of these evils, and the *titulus*, *Superbia*, is located directly beneath Eve's feet. To Adam's side of the tree sits a man with a money bag who is labeled *Dives avarus*, while to Eve's side sits a man labeled *Pauper superbus*. [20] The greedy Adam, associated with the rich miser Dives, must now work for his food; the fallen Eve is linked to the proud pauper, a peasant enthroned as a mock king holding a sickle in place of a real scepter. While the San Marco mosaic avoids referring to Adam as avaricious, it clearly mocks the proud but fallen Eve.

Another basis for Eve's power over the postlapsarian Adam is carnal lust, for, as Pope Innocent III explains in his scathing condemnation of human earthly existence, *On the Misery of the Human Condition* of about 1195, "lust makes the mind effeminate" [21]—that is, weakens its power to reason. This ability to control Adam reflects Eve's imputed power prior to the Fall, and God's condemnation of Eve to desire Adam reinforces it in her postlapsarian character. Here, then, sits the seductive Eve, dressed in greater finery than Adam and newly ornamented and voluptuous following her expulsion. Her sudden change in costume—we recall how she and Adam appeared virtually identical as God propelled them out of

FIGURE 29.

Labors of Adam and Eve,
Speculum humanae
salvationis, Flemish,
c. 1485–95, Paris,
Bibliothèque nationale,
ms. fr. 6275, fol. 4r.

Eden—represents her lustful nature, confirmed by the similar dress of two other females in the San Marco atrium mosaics, both also associated with sex and seduction: Hagar and Potiphar's wife. Hagar (Fig. 31) is the Egyptian slave given to Abraham to bear him a child when Sarah is unable to conceive. The mosaicists contrast her depiction sharply with that of the modest and well-covered Sarah by showing Hagar with a fillet in her uncovered hair and a belt under her clearly rounded breasts. In the Cotton Genesis, Sarah had also worn a fillet in uncovered hair, but it is eliminated by the thirteenth-century mosaicists, who attribute to her the demeanor and costume appropriate to thirteenth-century Venetian wives, who wore their hair covered. The contrast between these two women is heightened by their progeny, Hagar's son Ishmael, who is "born of the flesh" (Gal. 4:23) and father of the Arab nation, and Sarah's Isaac, born "by promise" (Gal. 4:23) and the second patriarch of the Hebrews.

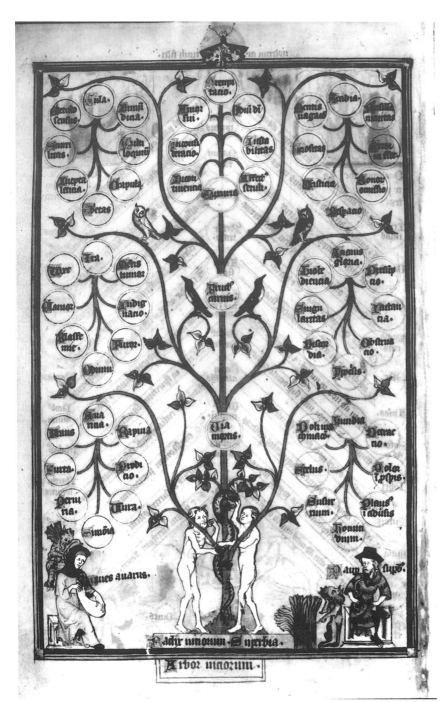

FIGURE 30.

Tree of Vices with Adam and Eve and personifications of Miserly Dives and The Proud Pauper, Psalter of Robert de Lisle, English, c. 1310, London, British Library, Arundel 83 II, fol. 128v.

70

FIGURE 31.

Abraham Handing
Hagar to Sarah, detail
of the Abraham cupola,
San Marco, Venice.

Potiphar's Egyptian wife (see Fig. 22), who tries to seduce Joseph and then falsely accuses him of wronging her, is more aristocratic and thus more highly ornamented. She wears a diadem in her exposed hair and has prominent breasts and a cross-legged pose we have already compared with Eve's following the Fall. By the later Middle Ages, the association of Muslim women with unbridled lust was a popular idea, and Venice in the age of the Crusades indulged in such anti-Muslim slurs.[22]

Eve's unveiled yet ornamented head is significant in other ways beyond demonstrating her carnality. It further illustrates her proud nature that still wishes to be like God and denies her submissiveness to Adam, another punishment—like that of laboring—that she chooses to ignore. The widespread medieval (not just Venetian) practice of women's veiling their heads was a significant social custom, for it reflected centuries of biblical exegesis focusing both on the Genesis command to be submissive and on Paul's own explanation of that text in I Corinthians 11 : 3 – 10 and elsewhere. Paul explicates the necessity of women's veiling their heads as resulting from Eve's sin and, more generally, relates it to womankind's seductiveness and pride; the veiling itself demonstrates appropriate submissiveness.[23]

Tertullian's "On the Apparel of Women," where he similarly identifies all women with Eve and goes so far as to attribute Christ's death on the Cross to Eve's sin, also discusses what he sees as typically female love of ornament and adornment. His remarks may be the source for the never fully explained medieval attribute of spindle and distaff for Eve.[24]

> *You* are the devil's gateway: *you* are the unsealer of that (forbidden) tree: *you* are the first deserter of the divine law: *you* are she who persuaded him whom the devil was not valiant enough to attack. *You* destroyed so easily God's image man. On account of *your* desert—that is, death—even the Son of God had to die. And do you think about adorning yourself over and above your tunic of skins? Come, now; if from the beginning of the world the Milesians sheared sheep, and the Serbians spun trees, and the Tyrians dyed, and the Phrygians embroidered with the needle, and the Babylonians with the loom, and pearls gleamed, and onyx stones flashed; if gold itself also had already issued, with the cupidity (which accompanies it), from the ground; if the mirror too, already had license to lie so largely, Eve, expelled from paradise (Eve) already dead, would also have coveted *these* things, I imagine! . . . these things are the baggage of woman in her condemned and dead state, instituted as if to swell the pomp of her funeral. . . . Female habit carries with it a twofold idea—dress and ornament. By "dress" we mean what they call "womanly gracing"; by "ornament," what is suitable should be called "womanly *dis*gracing." . . . Against the one we lay the charge of ambition, against the other prostitution.[25]

This passage, written in the early church but its sentiments not forgotten by the thirteenth century, stereotypes all women as vain and worldly, and the San Marco *Labors* confirms Tertullian's suspicions about Eve. There may even be a pun here on the word *kosmos*, which means both "ornament" and "world."[26] In her desire for power, the worldly Eve ornaments herself beyond her "tunic of skins" and, in so doing, usurps once again the role of the Creator, the first fashioner of garments. Perhaps the scene of God clothing Adam and Eve, rare in medieval art but found at San Marco, was included to remind the viewer of Eve's initial clothing, simple but created by God himself, that she so quickly rejects. Her distaff and spindle reveal that she will create new clothes—from the wool of the animals above?—to make her newly worldly self yet more attractive and powerful. Her pointed sidelong glance at Adam will entrap him further, as eyes were understood in the Middle Ages to emanate rays rather than to receive them.[27] Ignoring God's command to labor and to be submissive, Eve instead enacts the punishment that Jerome omitted in his translation: she glances at Adam and desires him. Her twisted posture expresses her sinful and seductive nature, and, having discarded God's plain tunic of skins, her body appears suddenly voluptuous. Adam is turned away from her now, focused on his labor, but that she will successfully allure him is confirmed by the scene immediately below of Adam in bed with her, his left hand on her breast (see Fig. 28).

It should not surprise us that what the mosaics suggest about Eve are exactly the characteristics imputed to women in general in thirteenth-century Venice, as confirmed by other primary documents. Laws were written and customs established with the clear presupposition that women were defective, proud and unsubmissive, vain and lustful; for men, marriage to them was necessary, but also dangerous.[28] The Venetian Franciscan Fra' Paolino, writing his *Del governo della famiglia* in Venice in the opening years of the fourteenth century, shortly after the atrium mosaics were finished, describes women in a highly formulaic way that is at least partly based on commonplaces about Eve. Noting that a wife "è molto defetosa en l'anema" ("highly defective in her soul"), he describes her as naturally unstable, quarrelsome, timorous, and prone to change her mind.[29] Further, she is an impediment to her husband's attention to wisdom. As Pope Innocent III had advised a century earlier, "She wants to master, and will not be mastered. She will not be a servant, *she* must be in charge. She must have a finger in everything. . . . So the burden of marriage is heavy indeed."[30]

Beauty and vanity, and their subsequent manifestation as concupiscence, were of special concern to late medieval moralists, and Innocent and Fra' Paolino were no exceptions. The former writes:

> The wife insists on having precious jewels and a huge wardrobe, so that her attire often costs more than her husband's salary; but otherwise she sighs and

weeps, babbles and murmurs day and night. . . . If she be beautiful, men readily go after her; if she be ugly, she goes as readily after them.[31]

Fra' Paolino warns that beauty should not be her only virtue, for in reality, it is a danger. Citing Aristotle, whose works were widely read in the thirteenth century, Fra' Paolino states, "ella satrova plu prona po a carnal concupisentia" ("she finds herself more prone to carnal licentiousness").[32] Even Venetian law reflected these gender assumptions. Fourteenth-century Venetian criminal records indicate that women and men were tried differently for sex crimes,[33] and sumptuary laws regulating women's dress had already been passed in Venice as early as 1299. The expansion of these female-oriented codes in 1334 was possibly in direct response to Fra' Paolino's plea regarding the wife's excessive vanity:

> While the husband takes trouble to satisfy her with everything in fashion, as costly garments, gold, precious stones, servants, and household goods, she is still full of lamentations, and says, "That woman is better dressed than I am— that other woman is more honoured than I am. . . ." Sometimes the man follows too much the will of the woman in buying her ornaments, and this gives rise to much evil, excessive expenditure, and the woman is more than ever filled with pride, and for vainglory desires still more to go out and show herself. Therefore the man should dress his wife as he thinks right, and according to the manner which prevails among his equals. And if the custom of the city in this respect is extravagant, it should be regulated by laws after the manner of the Romans.[34]

Sumptuary laws enacted in Venice throughout the late Middle Ages and Renaissance aimed repeatedly at women's hair ornaments, dress, and jewelry. The codes were enforced by the Signori di Notte, a group established by the mid-thirteenth century, just at the time when many such social regulations concerning the body, particularly applying to a variety of groups of "others"—women, Jews, homosexuals, Muslims—were decreed.[35] Similarly, preachers of the time inveighed against women's vanity and lust, believing Eve's weaknesses and strengths to be those of all women.[36] The characterization of Eve in the mosaics is understood to be universal, and she sits in the cupola as a warning for all who see her from below.

Mortal Life below the Cupola

The final two scenes of Adam and Eve's story appear in the east lunette (see Fig. 28), followed by the story of their children, Cain and Abel (see

Fig. 3). It is meaningful that the gaze of the viewer drops from the scenes of Eden in the cupola above to the upper wall lunettes supporting the vault. Four cherubim, as we have seen, located in the pendentives of the dome between the lunettes and the cupola, guard that more holy Edenic space from Adam and Eve's descendants below—Cain and Abel, Noah, and so on—but also from us, the viewers in the narthex. A further sign that we have left the Garden is the setting; human-made and even feminine, it is the circumscribed interior world of women, the bedroom of conception and birth. Eve and Adam's role as progenitors dominates and is publicly acknowledged, just as the mosaics earlier had intimated.

The Latin *titulus* above the *Conception of Cain* (Fig. 28, left side), once again abbreviated from the Vulgate, is unusual in two regards. First, it is the "Increase and multiply, and fill the earth" dictum spoken by God (using an *ait* formula) immediately following the P-text creation of the bisexual human creature (Gen. 1:28) and so is significantly removed from its proper context. Second, the figure of the Creator is omitted, although his commanding speech is included.[37] His omission may be explained by the fact that the text that logically fits the episode in the visual narrative, "And Adam knew Eve his wife" (Gen. 4:1), does not call for the figure of the Deity, and the Cotton Genesis model would not have included him in its miniature; it is also likely that the obvious carnality of the scene precluded his presence. However, the reason for the textual substitution originates in the church's struggle with the heretical Cathars, even though that exhortation to procreate is largely subverted by the image.

The mosaic of Cain's conception demonstrates well the ambivalence felt in the late Middle Ages toward procreation, particularly in light of the raging dualist Catharist heresy of the time. On the one hand, there is the church's centuries-old distrust of the body and carnality; on the other, the ecclesiastical authorities in the early thirteenth century found themselves in the awkward position of needing to counter the Catharist conviction that *all* intercourse was by nature evil. Peter Comestor had already addressed this problem in his widely known text,[38] but it was still an issue when Pope Innocent III, ardently antiheretical, wrote *On the Misery of the Human Condition*. Even though stridently Neoplatonic in his favoring of the metaphysical over the physical, and dualist in many of his perspectives, Innocent narrowly offers arguments against the more extreme Cathars. He and the subsequent Fourth Lateran Council of 1215, which codified many

of the church's positions with regard to carnal matters, advocated the orthodox position that God's command, "Increase and multiply, and fill the
earth" (Gen. 1:28), justified sexual intercourse.[39] Marriage and procreation were thus sanctioned by the church.

That the San Marco mosaicists altered the image-text relationship to
juxtapose this divine command with Adam's and Eve's initial act of carnal
intercourse was thus no small matter. The text was prominently invoked
in the early thirteenth century as an anti-Catharist justification for marriage, and the mosaicists here properly assert their orthodoxy. However,
the mosaics project the same ambivalent message asserted by Innocent's
almost contemporaneous diatribe. Visually, Adam's and Eve's fallen and
bestial natures are evident as they both abandon any pretense of identity
with the divine and assume the position of the "two-headed" overlapping
pairs of beasts in earlier scenes (see Plate 5 and Fig. 7). Their closed eyes
and recumbent postures remind the viewer of Adam's sleep during Eve's
fateful creation and Noah's drunkenness (see Plate 7 and Fig. 14); further,
the patristic association of sleep with susceptibility to sensual delights,
noted above, persisted in late medieval Italy. As Innocent himself wrote,
"In carnal intercourse the mind's clarity is put to sleep."[40] Like the
miscreant Eve, the child they produce is animal-natured and ruled by
passion.[41] While following the general composition of the Cotton Genesis
model, the mosaicists both alter and emphasize the *left*-hand gestures, so
crucial to the visual representation of blatant carnality and loss of reason
in the scene at San Marco.[42] We do see confirmed here that Adam was
Cain's father, for the question of paternity and the possible adultery of Eve
with Satan was another long-standing controversy. Paradoxically, however, the text offers divine sanction for this dangerous act, reminding
viewers, after these many warnings against carnality, of their Christian
duty regarding marriage and procreation.[43] Human conception is ultimately part of God's world, not initiated by some force of evil outside the
Deity's control.[44]

The Cotton Genesis illustrates four additional scenes depicting Adam
and/or Eve, but at San Marco, only the *Birth of Abel* (see Fig. 28) is included. This revision again reveals thirteenth-century attitudes, for it further discredits Eve's character by eliminating the final two speeches of the
total of four allotted to her in the Bible—one when she names Cain and
another when she does the same for Seth—and by omitting the event that

shows her most reconciled with God, the birth of Seth.[45] Although the *Birth of Abel* has been completely remade since the thirteenth century, the composition is probably faithful to the original.[46] We can see that the story of the first parents ends as it began, with Adam standing erect at the picture's right, holding and thus associated with the son who represents reason and faithfulness to God, while Eve lies at the picture's left,[47] allied with the evil Cain. Cain's attributes of a cup and an emptied wineskin corroborate his (and Eve's) sense-ruled nature.[48] Orthodox theology would assert, however, that Eve is redeemable, as yet another line of reasoning in the medieval exegesis of the Genesis Creation text affirms. Paul, in I Timothy 2:8–15, summarizes the various defects of women, exhorting them to be modest, submissive, and silent, and ends with a reference to Adam and Eve and the reassurance that the "woman shall be saved by childbearing."[49] However, the mosaicists seem not to acknowledge that her curse shall become her salvation.

This lengthy exploration of Adam and Eve's fate after they leave Eden reveals the enormity of their sin and its consequences for human history. We see that Adam is a changed man. Where once he stood erect in the image of the Creator, he is now bent low by mortal existence with its physical labor and sexual intercourse. Only in his final scene is he restored to his upright stance at the picture's right. *His* story conforms to a developmental tale of initial perfection, fall from grace, penance, and redemption. With the help of the New Adam, he will regain his initial perfection. Eve's story is more complex. Her initial imperfection causes the fall from grace, yet her ironic enthronement while Adam labors suggests neither penance nor submissiveness on her part to Adam's or God's will. Fashioned initially from Adam's rib, she has become the thorn in his side, ever ready to exert her power over him and cause him further ruin. Essentially unchanged from her prelapsarian self, Eve is still ruled by pride, disobedience, and her carnal nature. No wonder Thomas Aquinas struggles to explain that she will one day be Adam's equal in Paradise.[50] In the thirteenth century, man is the victim, woman the cause.

CHAPTER SIX

The Fallen World and
Thirteenth-Century Venice

These mosaics of Adam and Eve are tied inextricably to the fabric of thirteenth-century Venetian society. Located in San Marco, a building that represented the authority not just of religion but also of politics and the Venetian state, the mosaics reflect, for example, Venice's role as the New Rome and New Constantinople and her heightened connections both to the East and to the apostolic age of one of her most important patron saints, Mark; consequently, important Roman and Byzantine monuments and traditions from the first centuries of Christian art influenced the mosaicists.[1] Indeed, the late-fifth-century Cotton Genesis is an early Byzantine work and may have been stolen by Crusaders from Constantinople itself during the Fourth Crusade in 1204, or else acquired in Alexandria, the residence of St. Mark and the site of his martyrdom.[2] Similarly, the importance of St. Augustine as a theological source may relate to his association with the early Christian world.

The cupola narrative would also have functioned didactically by reinforcing the desired social codes in Venice; we have already seen evidence of this in chapter 5. However, other aspects of this can be explored, for example, through an examination of the abbreviated inscriptions located above each register of mosaics. These *tituli* are legible to literate viewers standing below, albeit in the thirteenth century such people would have been both few in number and mostly male. However, the role of the *tituli* was significant, for they probably functioned as prompts for preachers using the mosaics as visual exempla for the faithful. Thus we can obtain from them a sense of the most basic information to be imparted to the illiterate public. The *tituli* are also important in this study because only some were copied from the Vulgate, while others were produced, so far as we know, as part of the thirteenth-century revision of the Creation story.

The nature of the didactic message is suggested by the abrupt change of form and alteration of tone in the Latin text accompanying the mosaics at a particularly significant moment in the narrative. Prior to the scene of Eve's temptation, the text above the mosaics consists of tersely abbreviated quotations taken directly from the Vulgate. More than half of them begin with the verb appropriate to the event below, usually the Creator's deed (e.g., "FIAT," "DIXIT," "FACIAMVS," "INSPIRAVIT") but in one case Adam's ("APELLAVITQVE ADAM"), and they therefore stress action. However, as we have seen, beginning with the text for the *Temptation of Eve* ("HIC SERPENS LOQVITVR EVE ET DECIPIT EAM") and continuing through the *Labors* and the inscription just above the four cherubim, the mosaics abandon the verb-driven abridgements from the Vulgate. Instead, all these texts begin with the demonstrative "HIC" ("Here"). This semantic construction—associated with oral discourse—reflects traditional classical rhetorical conventions used in courtroom situations by Cicero, for example, and reinforces the publicly judgmental and didactic aspects of this section of the mosaics.[3] Because it is self-consciously didactic in tone, it also both suggests the unknown author's assumption of an audience hearing the text while viewing the mosaics and interposes a controlling third party between that audience and the mosaics. Finally, "HIC" is both locative and temporal, and serves to focus the viewer's attention. Adam and Eve carry out the Fall here and now in the pictures but also here and now in our midst. Thus these scenes of Eve's and Adam's actions serve as exempla. It is as though with Eve's fateful conversation with the Serpent the viewer's earthly realm of place and time is firmly established. The voice now also sounds interpretive rather than simply narrative: the Serpent does not just speak to Eve (as in the Vulgate *dixit*) but deceives her, and so we find here an anticipation of the event's outcome, rather than its still innocent unfolding. The writer of the *tituli* for the mosaics, possibly identical with the overall planner of the pictorial cycle, recognized the important turn in the plot when the Serpent calls to Eve.

The didactic tone of the later *tituli* reinforces the emphasis on justice in the final four scenes of the cupola (see Figs. 24–26 and Plate 2), where God first accuses Adam and Eve of having sinned and then judges them, clothes them in their new mortality (one aspect of their punishment), and finally expels them from the Garden. Such a forensic approach, focusing on the justness of God's condemnation, typifies the scholastic attitude toward the Adam and Eve story.[4] But this preoccupation with the theme of justice is also evident in other of the narthex mosaics and on the west facade of the church, and at least partly originates in the political life of the thirteenth-century Venetian state.

Venice, which had in 1177 successfully negotiated the peace between Pope Alexander III and Emperor Frederick Barbarossa, considered Justice her chief virtue; as David Rosand has noted, in the course of the thirteenth century the city developed the iconography of personified Venice in the visual arts as well as in political thought, and Justice and Justitia were central to this myth and imagery.[5] It is not coincidental that precisely in the first half of the thirteenth century, when these mosaics were being worked on, Venetian law was significantly revised and codified. One result of these changes was a decrease in the Doge's real power and a consequent increase in the power of the Procurator. Interestingly, it was the first duty of this secular official, the Procurator, to supervise San Marco, including the overseeing of the mosaic and sculptural decoration, even down to seemingly insignificant particulars.

Given the participation of the Procurator, it is not surprising that the mosaics and sculptures of the west facade and atrium intermingle civic and religious themes, including those of secular and divine Justice. Unfortunately, the portal leading directly into the atrium below the Creation mosaics was altered in the fourteenth century, but the thirteenth-century central doorway into the atrium remains. Over that portal, although in restored form, is the most important example of divine Justice, the *Last Judgment* mosaic. While this subject traditionally graces thirteenth-century facades all over Europe, surrounding it at San Marco are civic images, specifically apotropaic reliefs of various of the city's protectors, including Sts. Demetrius and George and the Virgin Mary, but also the pagan Hercules.[6] The archivolts similarly combine sacred and profane imagery: there are—as identified by Demus—sculptures of the world before salvation, the Labors of the Months and the Zodiac, the Virtues and Beatitudes, and the Prophets and Christ. But additionally, there are "portraits" of the Venetian trades, with clear emphasis on local Venetian workers, the modern "Adams."

The narthex mosaics continue this interest in intermingling civic and divine Justice. For example, the viewer who stands under the Creation cupola and looks northward down the major axis of the narthex sees on the end wall a mosaic of the Judgment of Solomon. Demus calls this mosaic "the most conspicuous foreign body" in the atrium but then convincingly relates it to other references to justice in the mosaics of the north wing of the atrium, for example, in the scrolls of Habakkuk and Samuel, and to the personification of Justitia herself.[7] The inscriptions surrounding the image of Solomon and that over the adjacent Porta Sant'Alipio similarly celebrate Justice and admonish those who would betray it. Based on these *tituli* and images, Demus concludes that this area of the atrium might have functioned as a tribunal where an ecclesiastical court met and proposes that the practice began in the first half of the thirteenth century.

Extending Demus's ideas about the north wing of the atrium to the Creation cupola and other mosaics in the west wing, we see that these address issues of social and religious justice as well. Judgments resulting in acceptance or rejection of those who are worthy and those who are less so, of those who lead and those who submit, appear at the very beginning of the Old Testament mosaics, starting on Day One with the separation of Light and Darkness and of the good angels and the fallen ones. We have already seen how that theme of separation of the worthy and the less worthy is repeated by the creation of the naturally inferior Eve from Adam's side and her condemnation to be submissive to her superior spouse. This echoes once again in the distinctions between the just Abel and the fallen Cain. The story of Noah's drunkenness (see Fig. 14), unusually prominent in these mosaics, also results in a condemnation and separation of those who are worthy to rule and those who must submit. The sobered Noah curses Ham, the son who gazed on his nakedness and who will become the father of Canaan; Shem and Japhet, who covered his nakedness, are blessed and will rule over Ham. Centuries earlier Ambrose of Milan had already understood this biblical judgment to apply to human society on earth and to function as justification for the hierarchy of civic government.[8] Other descendants of Adam and Eve in the atrium mosaics reveal their natural superiority or their natural submissiveness and similarly serve to sanction behavior in thirteenth-century Venice. The tale of Jacob's son Joseph and his brothers repeats this theme of necessary separation, as does that of Abraham's children, Isaac and Ishmael. Ishmael's story was particularly relevant to thirteenth-century Venice, with the launching of the Fourth and Fifth Crusades in 1204 and 1217. As noted above, Ishmael was considered the father of the Muslim peoples, and his natural submissiveness justified the Crusaders' actions.

The extensiveness of this theme of admonition and Justice in the western atrium mosaics is further confirmed by later sculptures, based on these mosaics, located on the adjacent Doge's Palace directly to the south of the church. There subtle and complex intertwinings of state and religious iconography, echoing the far-reaching allusions within the Adam and Eve cupola and other atrium mosaics, are found in the sculptures on the three exposed corners. As Sinding-Larsen has demonstrated, these late-fourteenth- and early-fifteenth-century sculptures of the Drunkenness of Noah (paired with the archangel Raphael), the Judgment of Solomon (with Gabriel), and the Fall of Adam and Eve (with Michael, the archangel of the Last Judgment), along with a figure of Justitia at the center of the Piazzetta facade, create a unified program relating to Venice's identification with Justice and her concern for both divine law and human law.[9]

The mosaics function as visual documents and demonstrate their relevance not only to preaching and to civic, religious, and political ideas of justice but also to the liturgical functions of the church during the penitential season leading up to Easter. Adam and Eve are prominent in the exegetical literature of the Middle Ages but appear only infrequently in the liturgy. Where they do appear is in the immediately pre-Lenten and Lenten season, beginning on Septuagesima Sunday (the ninth Sunday before Easter, the third before Lent), and some of the expanded and even vernacular treatments of their story relate to that liturgy.[10] For Septuagesima Sunday, the Gospel reading is the story of the Prodigal Son (Luke 15), paired with the story of the Creation, Fall, and Expulsion. The liturgy for the ensuing weeks focuses on the forces of Darkness and Light, on spiritual battle, on the theme of the Babylonian Captivity, but also on the anticipated return to the Garden. Based on Augustinian ideas about the Seven Ages of the world, Old Testament texts are used for the Matins readings for the succeeding weeks and relate the stories of Noah (Sexagesima Sunday), Abraham (Quinquagesima Sunday), Joseph (the third Sunday in Quadragesima), and Moses (Laetare Sunday), the very narratives that follow the Creation cupola in the narthex at San Marco. Finally, Passion Sunday turns to the Babylonian Captivity and the laments of Jeremiah, while Maundy Thursday institutes the New Law of Christ.[11]

The inclusion of these Old Testament stories in the narthex may thus relate to Lenten practices widespread in Europe. Until the fourteenth century, penitents were dismissed from the church on Ash Wednesday as a reenactment of Adam and Eve's Expulsion from Paradise. At St. Lazarus in Autun, for example, penitents prostrated themselves on their hands and knees during the rite of public penance and exited the church through the north portal, below lintel sculptures of a prone Adam and Eve.[12] The southernmost portal on San Marco's west facade, with the cupola of Adam and Eve above, may well have functioned as a penitential portal. Penitents were readmitted to churches on Maundy Thursday, to begin their reconciliation at the time of Christ's sacrifice. Of course it is in the interior of San Marco, although there is no single mosaic program, that those relevant New Testament images of Mary and Christ and the Passion are found. Thus the Old Testament stories of the Fall, the Flood, the Wanderings, all narrating breaches between God and humans, are viewed in the ancillary entryways of the church, while the healing events of the coming of the second Adam and Eve and the promise of salvation are experienced inside the church proper. In this way we see again the mirrorlike function of the Genesis cupola. Viewers use the dome for the intensive examination of sin undertaken during the Lenten season. As they turn below it and follow the circuitous narrative, not only do they reenact the descent of the Fall, but they follow the "path of sinners," that is, "the wicked walk around in a circle" (Ps. 11:9).[13] To find redemption on Easter Sunday and symbolically return to the Garden, they will need to ready their souls by Maundy Thursday's return to the interior of the church to mirror those depictions of the divine; symbolically, their purified souls return once again to being in the image of the Deity.[14]

The implied circular motion of the mosaics—actually experienced by

the viewer who turns while following the narrative from the floor below—
and their central moral of a fall suggest yet another allusion, to Fortune
and her Wheel. The shape of the cupola, with its horizontal registers and
vertical "spokes" of scene dividers, reiterates the wheel form familiarly
identified by visually literate thirteenth-century viewers as Fortune's
Wheel. Thematically the mosaics also correspond to multiple elements of
the twelfth-century literary tradition of "contempt of the world," in which
inconstancy plays a significant part. Linked to that tradition are major elements found in these mosaics, where Eve emerges "on top" in a world
turned upside down: the recognition of the corruption of the body and
natural order, the frailty of earthly existence and fickleness of women, the
devaluing of mundane things, and both the condemnation of existing social institutions and the promise of divine justice after death.[15] Of classical
origin, the theme of Fortune never totally died out in the Middle Ages,
particularly because of the popularity of Boethius's sixth-century *De consolatione philosophiae*, but a literary and visual revival of it in the twelfth
century resulted in the popular Wheel of Fortune sculptural groups over
church portals.[16] The complexities of its literary tradition are not of
importance here, for these would be unknown to most Venetian citizens, yet the theme's widespread inclusion in didactic literature, where
Fortune's Wheel represents the mutability and instability of the world,
makes it an appropriate cautionary subject for this public site. Typical
images (Fig. 32), whether in private manuscripts or on public facades,
include a wheel encircled by male rulers, at the center of which is an enthroned or standing personification of Dame Fortune. At the top sits or
stands a king, on one side of the wheel a ruler begins to topple, at the
bottom lies a fallen one, and at the other side ascends a fourth. In some
cases, Latin inscriptions clarify their status: *regno* for the figure at the top,
followed by *regnavi, sum sine regno,* and *regnabo.*[17]

It is ironic that the circle, when representing a turning wheel, can em-
body instability and commotion but can alternatively and even simultaneously signify the stable eternity of God's perfection and the cosmic order
of his Creation. The later Christian Middle Ages conflated those seemingly inconsistent ideas about that singular form—along with others about
free will and divine omnipotence—and came to a new understanding of
the meaning of Fortune. In this way, fate could be viewed as not entirely
capricious but rather as an instrument of divine providence, operating

FIGURE 32.

Wheel of Fortune,
Carmina Burana,
Kärnten or South
Tyrol, mid-thirteenth
century, Munich,
Bayerische
Staatsbibliothek,
Clm 4660, fol. 1r.

within the narratives of the Old Testament, for example. Thus, appended in the twelfth century to a ninth-century manuscript on Job, whose misfortunes were understood to be inflicted by God, is a drawing of Fortune and her Wheel.[18]

The San Marco mosaics synthesize similar ideas of divine order with the commotion and foolishness of human action.[19] On the one hand, the concentric circles are cosmic representations of the initial perfection of God's Creation, reiterated by the symbolic Dome of Heaven of the architectural form itself. Yet, as the tale of the first parents so well demonstrates, free will allows for the possibility of error—of the Fall. Thus the appropriateness of Fortune's Wheel for Adam and Eve and their descendants is apparent. Like their story, the allegory of Fortune involves a cyclical view of human history as a series of ascents and falls. We are to learn from the faulty behavior of the Old Adam and Eve yet rest assured that they will be supplanted and redeemed by the New; Fortune, admonishing and moralizing, promises ruin yet also offers hope. Finally, the microcosmic quality of the circular fashioning of the San Marco narrative imparts a macrocosmic sense of its relevance for all human activity.

Artists outside Venice also recognized the efficacy of conflating Fortune with the Creation story, as demonstrated in the early-fourteenth-century Holkham Bible Picture Book. There, *Fortune's Wheel* (Fig. 33) is juxtaposed with the miniature that commences the Genesis Creation cycle, *God in the Act of Creation with His Compass* (Plate 12). The circularity of Fortune's Wheel and her central location echo the cosmic circles of God's Creation and his centrality. Interestingly, a secondary theme in this miniature helps explain why Fortune herself would be present "in the beginning." Above the figure of the enthroned God is a proud Lucifer enthroned, and angels sit to either side of him. Those to his right dutifully ignore Lucifer by turning their backs; those to his sinister left, however, adore him rather than God. Thus we see here a reiteration of the Augustinian interpretation that, at the very beginning of Creation, the rebellious angels were separated from the enlightened ones. The Wheel of Fate, however, as an instrument of divine providence and assurance of God's omnipotence, has already begun to turn. Lucifer will fall and a Hell mouth awaits him below the figure of God.

The Hildesheim *Missal* of about 1159 also conflates these themes of Fortune and God's Creation and recognizes Eve as literally central to

Fortune. The manuscript includes a full-page miniature of the *Fall of the Rebel Angels* along with *The Lord Holding the Wheel of Creation*.[20] In the latter, the Creator displays a wheel containing images of the six days of Creation; in the center, the place most commonly occupied by the figure of the standing or enthroned Fortune, appears Eve's birth from Adam's side. Below the Wheel, in the area usually reserved for those who have fallen into ill fortune, are the scenes of Adam and Eve's Expulsion and Cain's murder of Abel. In this miniature, Eve's creation is central to the unfolding narrative of the Fall, and her location identifies her with Dame or Queen Fortune herself. Further, the separation of the good archangel Michael from the rebel Lucifer in the *Fall of the Rebel Angels* once again parallels Eve's separation from Adam's side and the angelic fall from grace.

In the San Marco mosaics, although Eve's creation is similarly climactic to the narrative, it is unclear whether Eve's regal posture at her "labors" deliberately suggests Queen Fortune. Supporting the allusion are several elements, for example, Eve's enthroned posture, her gender (Fortune herself is always female, but her victims in this age are typically male), and her attributes of a distaff and spindles. Such spinning implements belonged to the three classical Fates who wove human destiny; the capriciousness of that trio was expressed by their ability to snip the thread of life at any time. While the three Fates were one of many classical themes that remained alive in the Middle Ages, spindles and distaff were not widely associated with Lady Fortune in the thirteenth century; however, by the fourteenth century, Boccaccio identifies one of the classical Fates, Lachesis, with Fortune, and spinning implements become more common as Fortune's attributes.[21] Thus it is possible that we are to identify Eve with Dame Fortune herself. Alternatively, Eve could simply represent one of the players in Fortune's game; she sits enthroned in the *regno* posture, formulaically on "top," while exactly opposite her, at the "bottom" of the cupola, is the upside-down scene of Adam and Eve's fall, in *sum sine regno* position. It will not be until after the Incarnation makes salvation possible that Adam and Eve will finally be able to find redemption.[22]

Whoever planned the Creation cycle at San Marco synthesized a remarkable number of visual and written texts, including those of contemporary theologians, and was sensitive to local devotions and the mores of contemporary Venetian society, with its notions of appropriate gender roles based on the God-given natures of men and women. This kind of richness of meaning is not at all foreign to medieval art, for the very success of didactic imagery depends on its ability to reach a disparate audience, each member of which brings different visual memories and religious and civic knowledge to it. Thus it is appropriate that the "mirror" of the cupola reflects themes relating to theological issues, gender roles, and social codes of behavior, as well as the state itself.

The visual language of the mosaics is remarkably consistent and clear. While visual images are not productive in the same ways that written and spoken language is, by using syntax based on repetitions of patterns, compositions, gestures, postures, and colors, the mosaicists at San Marco reveal the fundamental relationship between Adam, Eve, and the Creator; for some kinds of messages—who is made in God's image?—they are less ambiguous than their discursive analogs. Reflecting and reinterpreting many verbal and visual sources, the creator of these mosaics offers a complex explanation for the Fall that equals those of contemporary exegetes.

It has long been recognized that Venice was experiencing renewed interest in its early Christian heritage and that the atrium mosaics exemplify this through their extensive dependence on the illuminations in the Cotton Genesis. What scholars have not sufficiently noted, however, are the consistently misogynist alterations made to the model's images by its thirteenth-century planner. Created within a religious and political world shaped by males, but aimed at a male and female audience, the mosaics express this didactic message through a powerful visual language that emphasizes likeness and difference. Its strident misogyny reflects the increasing hostility of thirteenth-century Europe toward the "other"—Muslim and Jew, homosexual and woman—and depicts Eve, the prototype and stereotype for all women, as flawed from the moment of her creation and unrepentant after her Fall. In so depicting her, the mosaicists address a fundamental question in Judeo-Christian theology regarding evil. They confirm that sin enters the world through a woman.

Excerpts from the Book of Genesis (Douay Version)

Chapter 1

1   In the beginning God created heaven, and earth.

2   And the earth was void and empty, and darkness was upon the face of the deep. And the spirit of God moved over the waters.

3   And God said: Be light made. And light was made.

4   And God saw the light that it was good; and he divided the light from the darkness.

5   And he called the light Day, and the darkness Night. And there was evening and morning one day.

6   And God said: Let there be a firmament made amidst the waters: and let it divide the waters from the waters.

7   And God made a firmament, and divided the waters that were under the firmament, from those that were above the firmament. And it was so.

8   And God called the firmament Heaven. And the evening and morning were the second day.

9   God also said: Let the waters that are under the heaven, be gathered together into one place, and let the dry land appear. And it was so done.

10   And God called the dry land Earth; and the gathering together of the waters, he called Seas. And God saw that it was good.

11   And he said: Let the earth bring forth the green herb, and such as may seed, and the fruit tree yielding fruit after its kind, which may have seed in itself upon the earth. And it was so done.

12   And the earth brought forth the green herb, and such as yieldeth seed according to its kind, and the tree that beareth fruit, having seed each one according to its kind. And God saw that it was good.

13   And the evening and the morning were the third day.

14   And God said: Let there be lights made in the firmament of heaven, to divide the day and the night, and let them be for signs, and for seasons, and for days and years:

15   To shine in the firmament of heaven, and to give light upon the earth. And it was so done.

16   And God made two great lights: a greater light to rule the day; and a lesser light to rule the night: and the stars.

17   And he set them in the firmament of heaven to shine upon the earth.

18   And to rule the day and the night, and to divide the light and the darkness. And God saw that it was good.

19   And the evening and morning were the fourth day.

20   God also said: Let the waters bring forth the creeping creature having life, and the fowl that may fly over the earth under the firmament of heaven.

21   And God created the great whales, and every living and moving creature, which the waters brought forth, according to their kinds, and every winged fowl according to its kind. And God saw that it was good.

22   And he blessed them, saying: Increase and multiply, and fill the waters of the sea; and let the birds be multiplied upon the earth.

23   And the evening and the morning were the fifth day.

24   And God said: Let the earth bring forth the living creature in its kind, cattle and creeping things, and beasts of the earth, according to their kinds. And it was so done.

25   And God made the beasts of the earth according to their kinds, and cattle, and every thing that creepeth on the earth after its kind. And God saw that it was good.

26   And he said: Let us make man to our image and likeness; and let him have dominion over the fishes of the sea, and the fowls of the air, and the beasts, and the whole earth, and every creeping creature that moveth upon the earth.

27   And God created man to his own image; to the image of God he created him. Male and female he created them.

28   And God blessed them, saying: Increase and multiply, and fill the

earth, and subdue it, and rule over the fishes of the sea, and the fowls of the air, and all living creatures that move upon the earth.

29 And God said: Behold I have given you every herb bearing seed upon the earth, and all trees that have in themselves seed of their own kind, to be your meat:

30 And to all beasts of the earth, and to every fowl of the air, and to all that move upon the earth, and wherein there is life, that they may have to feed upon. And it was so done.

31 And God saw all the things that he had made, and they were very good. And the evening and morning were the sixth day.

Chapter 2

1 So the heavens and the earth were finished, and all the furniture of them.

2 And on the seventh day God ended his work which he had made: and he rested on the seventh day from all his work which he had done.

3 And he blessed the seventh day, and sanctified it: because in it he had rested from all his work which God created and made.

4 These are the generations of the heaven and the earth, when they were created, in the day that the Lord God made the heaven and the earth:

5 And every plant of the field before it sprung up in the earth, and every herb of the ground before it grew: for the Lord God had not rained upon the earth and there was not a man to till the earth.

6 But a spring rose out of the earth, watering all the surface of the earth.

7 And the Lord God formed man of the slime of the earth, and breathed into his face the breath of life; and man became a living soul.

8 And the Lord God had planted a paradise of pleasure from the beginning: wherein he placed man whom he had formed.

9 And the Lord God brought forth of the ground all manner of trees, fair to behold, and pleasant to eat of: the tree of life also in the midst of paradise; and the tree of knowledge of good and evil.

10 And a river went out of the place of pleasure to water paradise, which from thence is divided into four heads.

11   The name of the one is Phison: that is it which compasseth all the land of Hevilath, where gold groweth.

12   And the gold of that land is very good: there is found bdellium, and the onyx stone.

13   And the name of the second river is Gehon: the same is it that compasseth all the land of Ethiopia.

14   And the name of the third river is Tigris: the same passeth along by the Assyrians. And the fourth river is Euphrates.

15   And the Lord God took man, and put him into the paradise of pleasure, to dress it, and to keep it.

16   And he commanded him, saying: Of every tree of paradise thou shalt eat:

17   But of the tree of knowledge of good and evil, thou shalt not eat. For in what day soever thou shalt eat of it, thou shalt die the death.

18   And the Lord God said: It is not good for man to be alone; let us make him a help like unto himself.

19   And the Lord God having formed out of the ground all the beasts of the earth, and all the fowls of the air, brought them to Adam to see what he would call them: for whatsoever Adam called any living creature the same is its name.

20   And Adam called all the beasts by their names, and all the fowls of the air, and all the cattle of the field: but for Adam there was not found a helper like himself.

21   Then the Lord God cast a deep sleep upon Adam: and when he was fast asleep, he took one of his ribs, and filled up flesh for it.

22   And the Lord God built the rib which he took from Adam into a woman: and brought her to Adam.

23   And Adam said: This now is bone of my bones, and flesh of my flesh; she shall be called woman, because she was taken out of man.

24   Wherefore a man shall leave father and mother, and shall cleave to his wife: and they shall be two in one flesh.

25   And they were both naked, to wit, Adam and his wife: and were not ashamed.

Chapter 3

1   Now the serpent was more subtle than any of the beasts of the earth which the Lord God had made. And he said to the woman: Why

hath God commanded you, that you should not eat of every tree of paradise?

2 And the woman answered him, *saying:* Of the fruit of the trees that are in paradise we do eat:

3 But of the fruit of the tree which is in the midst of paradise, God hath commanded us that we should not eat; and that we should not touch it, lest perhaps we die.

4 And the serpent said to the woman: No, you shall not die the death.

5 For God doth know that in what day soever you shall eat thereof, your eyes shall be opened: and you shall be as Gods, knowing good and evil.

6 And the woman saw that the tree was good to eat, and fair to the eyes, and delightful to behold: and she took of the fruit thereof, and did eat, and gave to her husband who did eat.

7 And the eyes of them both were opened: and when they perceived themselves to be naked, they sewed together fig leaves, and made themselves aprons.

8 And when they heard the voice of the Lord God walking in paradise at the afternoon air, Adam and his wife hid themselves from the face of the Lord God, amidst the trees of paradise.

9 And the Lord God called Adam, and said to him: Where art thou?

10 And he said: I heard thy voice in paradise and I was afraid, because I was naked, and I hid myself.

11 And he said to him: And who hath told thee that thou wast naked, but that thou hast eaten of the tree whereof I commanded thee that thou shouldst not eat?

12 And Adam said: The woman, whom thou gavest me to be my companion, gave me of the tree, and I did eat.

13 And the Lord God said to the woman: Why has thou done this? And she answered: The serpent deceived me, and I did eat.

14 And the Lord God said to the serpent: Because thou hast done this thing, thou art cursed among all cattle, and beasts of the earth. Upon thy breast shalt thou go, and earth shalt thou eat all the days of thy life.

15 I will put enmities between thee and the woman, and thy seed and her seed: she shall crush thy head, and thou shalt lie in wait for her heel.

16 To the woman also he said: I will multiply thy sorrows, and thy con-

ceptions. In sorrow shalt thou bring forth children, and thou shalt be under thy husband's power, and he shall have dominion over thee.

17 And to Adam he said: Because thou hast hearkened to the voice of thy wife, and hast eaten of the tree, whereof I commanded thee that thou shouldst not eat, cursed is the earth in thy work; with labour and toil shalt thou eat thereof all the days of thy life.

18 Thorns and thistles shall it bring forth to thee; and thou shalt eat the herbs of the earth.

19 In the sweat of thy face shalt thou eat bread till thou return to the earth, out of which thou wast taken: for dust thou art, and into dust thou shalt return.

20 And Adam called the name of his wife Eve: because she was the mother of all the living.

21 And the Lord God made for Adam and his wife garments of skins, and clothed them.

22 And he said: Behold Adam is become as one of us, knowing good and evil: now, therefore, lest perhaps he put forth his hand, and take also of the tree of life, and eat, and live for ever.

23 And the Lord God sent him out of the paradise of pleasure, to till the earth from which he was taken.

24 And he cast out Adam; and placed before the paradise of pleasure Cherubims, and a flaming sword, turning every way, to keep the way of the tree of life.

Chapter 4

1 And Adam knew Eve his wife: who conceived and brought forth Cain, saying: I have gotten a man through God.

2 And again she brought forth his brother Abel. And Abel was a shepherd, and Cain a husbandman.

3 And it came to pass after many days, that Cain offered, of the fruits of the earth, gifts to the Lord.

4 Abel also offered of the firstlings of his flock, and of their fat: and the Lord had respect to Abel, and to his offerings.

5 But to Cain and his offerings he had no respect: and Cain was exceedingly angry, and his countenance fell.

6 And the Lord said to him: Why art thou angry? And why is thy countenance fallen?

7   If thou do well, shalt thou not receive? But if ill, shall not sin forthwith be present at the door? But the lust thereof shall be under thee, and thou shalt have dominion over it.

8   And Cain said to Abel his brother: Let us go forth abroad. And when they were in the field, Cain rose up against his brother Abel, and slew him.

25   Adam also knew his wife again; and she brought forth a son, and called his name Seth, saying: God hath given me another seed, for Abel whom Cain slew.

Notes

Chapter One

1. There have been a number of new readings of the Hebrew Genesis text, e.g., P. Trible, "Depatriarchalizing in Biblical Interpretation" (1973), reprinted in *The Jewish Woman: New Perspectives*, ed. E. Koltun, New York, 1976, 217–40; M. Bal, "Sexuality, Sin, and Sorrow: The Emergence of Female Character (A Reading of Genesis 1–3)," in *The Female Body in Western Culture: Contemporary Perspectives*, ed. S. R. Suleiman, Cambridge, Mass., and London, 1986, 317–38; H. Bloom, *The Book of J*, with trans. by D. Rosenberg, New York, 1990, especially 27–28, 61–65, and 175–87 on Adam and Eve; and I. Pardes, *Countertraditions in the Bible: A Feminist Approach*, Cambridge, Mass., and London, 1992, who offers her own perspective but also summarizes and critiques six feminist readings of Genesis, including all those listed in this note.

2. J. M. Evans, *"Paradise Lost" and the Genesis Traditions*, Oxford, 1968, discusses many of these versions of the Genesis text prior to the seventeenth century. For a listing of Genesis narratives from the early modern and modern world, consult R. Couffignal, *Le drame de l'Eden. Le récit de la Genèse et sa fortune littéraire*, Toulouse, 1980.

3. With regard to Jerome's translations and gender issues, see J. Barr, "The Vulgate Genesis and Jerome's Attitude towards Women" (1982), reprinted in *Equally in God's Image*, ed. J. Holloway, C. S. Wright, and J. Bechtold, New York, 1990, 122–28, and her "Influence of St. Jerome on Medieval Attitudes to Women," in *After Eve: Women in the Theology of the Christian Tradition*, ed. J. M. Soskice, London, 1990, 89–102.

4. This group is known as the Cotton Genesis recension, a family of works that are all related to a now-lost visual source, probably a manu-

script (or several manuscripts) identical or nearly identical to the late-fifth-century Cotton Genesis (London, British Library, Cod. Cotton Otho B. VI.). Consult K. Weitzmann and H. Kessler's monumental study, *The Cotton Genesis*, Princeton, 1986, 16–29, for a discussion and listing of these important Genesis images. My conclusions are highly indebted to the scholarship of Weitzmann and Kessler, whose reconstruction of the now virtually destroyed Cotton Genesis was instrumental to my study; O. Demus's work on San Marco and Venice has been equally valuable.

5. J. H. Morey, "Peter Comestor, Biblical Paraphrase, and the Medieval Popular Bible," *Speculum* 68 (1993): 6–35, discusses the popularity of this version of the biblical text, composed c. 1170, and its "canonical" authority in the thirteenth century. The full Latin text is found in J. P. Migne, *Patrologiae cursus completus*, Series latina, Paris, 1844–64, 198: 1049–1722 (hereafter PL).

6. Art historians need not be so dependent on finding written textual sources for what is clear visual information. Leo Steinberg, throughout *The Sexuality of Christ*, New York, 1983, addresses this issue extensively.

7. Bal, in her discussion of narratology and the Genesis text in "Sexuality, Sin, and Sorrow," 319, defines the *retrospective fallacy* as consisting of "the projection of an accomplished, singular and named character-image on previous textual elements which *lead* to the construction of that character." I adopt her term because it parallels my observations here regarding visual narrative. There has been criticism of this term, for example, by Pardes, *Countertraditions*, 32.

8. One can hardly begin to cite all the relevant work done on this question in recent literature, but particularly useful overviews and extensive bibliographies can be found in W. J. T. Mitchell, *Iconology: Image, Text, Ideology*, Chicago and London, 1986; M. Iversen, "Vicissitudes of the Visual Sign," *Word and Image* 6 (1990): 212–16; and M. Bal and N. Bryson, "Semiotics and Art History," *Art Bulletin* 73 (1991): 174–208. Works that relate these ideas more specifically to medieval art include M. Schapiro, *Words and Pictures*, The Hague, 1973; M. Camille, "Seeing and Reading: Some Visual Implications of Medieval Literacy and Illiteracy," *Art History* 8 (1985): 26–49, and idem, "The Book of Signs: Writing and Visual Difference in Gothic Manuscript Illumination," *Word and Image* 1 (1985): 133–48; H. L. Kessler, "Reading Ancient and Medieval Art," *Word and Image* 5, no. 1 (1989): 1 (the entire issue dedicated to this question is edited by Kessler); L. G. Duggan, "Was Art Really the 'Book of the Illiterate'?" *Word and Image* 5 (1989): 227–51; and R. Brilliant, "The Bayeux Tapestry: A Stripped Narrative for Their Eyes and Ears," *Word and Image* 7 (1991): especially 108–14.

9. *The Gothic Idol: Ideology and Image-Making in Medieval Art*, Cambridge, 1989, 162.

10. *The Church of San Marco in Venice*, Washington, D.C., 1960, 135. Some have proposed that Joachim of Fiore, an influential preacher and writer who possibly visited Venice in the late twelfth century, may have influenced the program, but Demus, *The Mosaics of San Marco in Venice*, 2 vols., Chicago and London, 1984, 2:97, remains skeptical.

11. Demus, *Church of San Marco*, 52–53.

Chapter Two

1. These dates are Demus's (*Mosaics of San Marco*, 2:4 and 2:72), while Weitzmann and Kessler, *The Cotton Genesis*, 18, suggest c. 1220–75.

2. Johan Jakob Tikkanen, *Die Genesismosaiken von S. Marco in Venedig u. Ihr Verhältniss zu den Miniaturen der Cottonbibel*, Acta societatis scientiarum fennicae, vol. 17, Helsinki, 1889. See Weitzmann and Kessler for a reconstruction of this important manuscript as well as an account of its history and opinions regarding style and attribution (3–7 and 30–34).

3. All the inscriptions are transcribed in Demus, *Mosaics of San Marco*, 2:76–79; Latin *tituli* quoted here are taken from Demus and will not be noted individually. It is significant that the *tituli* are from the Vulgate, for the text of the Cotton Genesis itself is a Greek translation of the Old Latin text. My comparisons are thus to the Vulgate.

4. Recent writers on visual narratives have stressed the importance of the viewer's already knowing the basic story prior to viewing the art. See, for example, R. Brilliant, *Visual Narratives: Storytelling in Etruscan and Roman Art*, Ithaca, N.Y., and London, 1984, 29, 52, and 69, and M. A. Lavin, *The Place of Narrative: Mural Decoration in Italian Churches, 431–1600*, Chicago and London, 1990, 6. There have been other interesting studies regarding pictorial narrative published recently that pertain in a general way to the issues at hand here. See, for example, the ten essays in vol. 16 of Studies in the History of Art, National Gallery of Art, Washington, D.C., 1985, ed. H. L. Kessler and M. S. Simpson, entitled collectively *Pictorial Narrative in Antiquity and the Middle Ages*, as well as M. Kupfer's *Romanesque Wall Painting in Central France: The Politics of Narrative*, New Haven and London, 1993. Regarding verbal illiteracy, another topic of extensive scholarly interest, consult the important study by F. H. Bäuml, "Varieties and Consequences of Medieval Literacy and Illiteracy," *Speculum* 55 (1980): 237–65; the articles cited above by Camille and Duggan; and W. J. Diebold, "Verbal, Visual, and Cultural Literacy in Medieval Art: Word and Image in the Psalter of Charles the Bald," *Word and Image* 8 (1992): 89–99.

5. B. Bertoli, *I mosaici di San Marco*, Milan, 1986, 56.

6. See M. Friedman, "More on 'Right' and 'Left' in Painting," *Assaph: Studies in Art History* 5 (1980): 123–30, and below, chap. 3 n. 7.

7. J.-C. Schmitt, "The Rationale of Gestures in the West: Third to Thirteenth Centuries," in *A Cultural History of Gesture*, ed. J. Bremmer and H. Roodenburg, Ithaca, N.Y., 1992, 59.

8. The literature on semiotics and the visual arts is too broad to list here, but with regard to gestures and their meaning in medieval art, consult J.-C. Schmitt, *La raison des gestes dans l'occident médiéval*, Paris, 1990, wherein he analyzes at length medieval theories of gesture, and his edited volume *Gestures, History and Anthropology* 1 (1984), including his "Introduction and General Bibliography," 1–23, wherein he offers an excellent overview of his ideas; and *A Cultural History of Gesture*, ed. J. Bremmer and H. Roodenburg, Ithaca, N.Y., 1992. F. Garnier, *Le langage de l'image au Moyen Age*, 2d ed., Paris, 1982, is less useful.

9. This type is based on the Creator figures found in the Cotton Genesis. See K. Weitzmann, "The Genesis Mosaics of San Marco and the Cotton Genesis Miniatures," in Demus, *Mosaics of San Marco*, 2:109.

10. See details of the gestures in the Babel scene in Demus, *Mosaics of San Marco*, 2: pls. 183 and 189–92. Left hands are generally not used by figures in the atrium mosaics, but they do function significantly in a number of scenes. For example, Potiphar's wife (2: pl. 268) catches hold of Joseph's garment with her left hand as she tries to seduce him, and in the *Hospitality of Abraham* (2: colorpl. 51), Sarah is seen through the opening of the tent behind the three holy visitors, her left hand prominent and her right hand unseen. According to Gen. 18:12–15, Sarah at this moment in the narrative lies to God when she denies having laughed. Another rare avoidance of right-hand gestures for speech is found in *Moses with Two Hebrews* (2: pl. 320), where the Hebrews argue with left-hand gestures, and Moses admonishes them with his left hand raised in speech.

11. Camille, "Seeing and Reading," 27–28, especially n. 11, discusses the origins of this rhetorical gesture.

12. Aristotle in his *Categories*, chap. 10, discusses four types of contraries: correlative opposites, contraries, positive and privative terms, and contradictories.

13. Augustine's importance for the Creation cupola may be due to two particular factors. Venice in the thirteenth century was interested in her role as the New Rome and New Constantinople, and thus was particularly responsive to creating ties to the early Christian world, of which Augustine was a part. O. Demus first discussed this as a widespread Venetian Gothic phenomenon in "A Renascence of Early Christian Art in Thirteenth-Century Venice," in *Late Classical and Mediaeval Studies in Honor of Albert Mathias Friend, Jr.*, Princeton, 1955, 348–61.

14. See S. E. Schreiner, "Eve, the Mother of History: Reaching for the Reality of History in Augustine's Later Exegesis of Genesis," in *Gene-

sis 1–3 in the History of Exegesis, ed. G. A. Robbins, Lewiston, N.Y., and Queenston, Ont., 1988, 140–42, and M.-T. D'Alverny, "Les anges et les jours," *Cahiers archéologiques* 9 (1957): 271–78.

15. For example in his *City of God* 11.9, 11.22–24, and 12.2–3. Aquinas discusses the origin of evil and its relationship to good in his *Summa theologica* pt. I, qq. 48 and 49.

16. B. J. Bamberger, *Fallen Angels*, Philadelphia, 1952, 201.

17. Augustine, *City of God* 11.19, trans. M. Dods, New York, 1950, 362. Augustine particularly discusses the fallen angels in 11.9, 11.11, and 11.19. The artworks in the Cotton Genesis recension have been studied closely with regard to which day the creation of the angels took place, for several traditions exist; consult D'Alverny, "Les anges et les jours," 274, and H. L. Kessler, "An Eleventh-Century Ivory Plaque from South Italy and the Cassinese Revival," *Jahrbuch der Berliner Museen* 8 (1966): 80–83. While San Marco's Day One has been associated by some authors with that Creation, and E. Borsook notes that at Monreale the angels are created on Day One as personifications of enlightenment (*Messages in Mosaic*, Oxford, 1990, 63 and n. 124), to my knowledge no one has suggested that the bicoloration of the angel at San Marco refers to both the good and the fallen angels. Weitzmann, in Demus, *Mosaics of San Marco*, 2 : 109, believes that the thirteenth-century San Marco mosaicists understood the winged figures to be angels rather than the personified days found in the original Cotton Genesis model.

18. Red and blue angels stand to Christ's dexter and sinister sides in the *Judgment of Nations*, a sixth-century mosaic at Sant'Apollinare Nuovo in Ravenna, a type for the Last Judgment. See E. Kirschbaum, "L'angelo rosso e l'angelo turchino," *Rivista di archeologia cristiana* 17 (1940): 209–27, for a detailed explanation of the use of red to indicate good angels and blue for the demonic, fallen angels, and the connections to Light and Darkness. Puzzlingly, this is the only instance in the San Marco cupola where the figure of the Creator has a halo outlined in blue rather than red.

19. Weitzmann and Kessler, *The Cotton Genesis*, 49–50, identify two trees in the manuscript as apple trees, and these seem to be the models for the two trees in the mosaic.

20. In all likelihood, this scene in the Cotton Genesis included a figure of the Creator, for this is a rare instance at San Marco of a *dixit* text (Gen. 1 : 20) not illustrated by the Creator in the active-agent pose. This folio (fol. 4) was missing from the Cotton Genesis prior to the fire of 1731 and may have been missing already in the thirteenth century. Weitzmann, in Demus, *Mosaics of San Marco*, 2 : 110, does not suggest whether or not the Creator figure was originally in the manuscript

miniature, but Weitzmann and Kessler, *The Cotton Genesis*, 50, note that the Salerno Antependium includes his figure (their fig. 15). The Cotton Genesis artists were extraordinarily interested in correlating each Genesis speech with a figure of the gesturing Creator.

21. Weitzmann, in Demus, *Mosaics of San Marco*, 2:111. The single aquatic bird near God's feet is adjacent to a badly damaged area, and a mate may have originally existed.

22. One unifying interpretation of the text is that this first human creature is actually bisexual and will be separated into two parts in Gen. 2:21–22. In general, the Jewish Talmudic scholars sustained this view (N. Aschkenasy, *Eve's Journey*, Philadelphia, 1986, 11), and some Kabbalah texts also understood it as a two-part creature, later literally sawn in half by the Deity (although the female who emerges from this process is usually identified with Lilith; see R. Patai, *The Hebrew Goddess*, rev. ed., New York, 1978, 192–93).

Peter Comestor, writing his *Historia scholastica* in about 1170, specifies that the first human creature was hermaphroditic (PL 198:1063). For other approaches to the ambiguity of Gen. 1:27, see R. R. Ruether, "Misogynism and Virginal Feminism in the Fathers of the Church," in *Religion and Sexism*, ed. R. R. Ruether, New York, 1974, 153–57; and for contemporary approaches to the text see (in addition to Trible, "Depatriarchalizing in Biblical Interpretation," 221–27, Aschkenasy, *Eve's Journey*, 9–14, and Bal, "Sexuality, Sin, and Sorrow," 320–26) R. Alter, *The Art of Biblical Narrative*, New York, 1981, 141–47, who discusses in general the P and J accounts and judges their combination to be a harmonious one; M. R. D'Angelo, "The Garden: Once and Not Again. Traditional Interpretations of Genesis 1:26–17 [*sic*] in I Corinthians 11:7–12," 1–41, and J. Milgrom, "Some Second Thoughts about Adam's First Wife," 225–53, both in *Genesis 1–3 in the History of Exegesis*, ed. G. A. Robbins, Lewiston, N.Y., and Queenston, Ont., 1988. Gen. 5:1–2 recapitulates Gen. 1, again using the term *adam*, not as a name, but as generic "humankind" consisting of both genders; see discussion in Pardes, *Countertraditions*, 55–56. The use of a plural pronoun for God in Gen. 1:26 was generally explained by Christian exegetes as a reference to the Trinity.

23. Weitzmann and Kessler, *The Cotton Genesis*, 51, suggest that fol. 5 (with the *Creation of the Terrestrial Animals* and the *Creation of Man*) was already missing by the thirteenth century. For their scene of the forming, the San Marco artists substituted the first illustration of the three used in the Cotton Genesis for the "second," or J-text, Creation (Gen. 2:7), the *Forming of Adam*. The second illustration (*Enlivenment of Adam*) was omitted entirely at San Marco, while the third part (*Animation of Adam*) is depicted at San Marco following the *Blessing of the Sev-*

enth Day. See the discussion of that *Animation* below. In the Vulgate, Gen. 2:7 initially uses the unsexed term *homo* for the creature made from clay, but by Gen. 2:19 this creature is called "Adam" (as a name, not the generic Hebrew term), and in Gen. 2:22 it is clearly "Woman" (*mulier*) who is pulled from Adam's side. Thus the clay creature was generally understood to be the male Adam.

24. Weitzmann, in Demus, *Mosaics of San Marco*, 2:112.

25. While scholars today have isolated two authors for the Genesis text, in the thirteenth century, Moses was identified as the single author. The mosaicists here recognized the discontinuity of the text, even if they did not distinguish the two writers at work.

26. This view was well established as early as the third century (E. Kono-witz, "The Program of the Carrand Diptych," *Art Bulletin* 66 [1984]: 486–87, discusses this in the early church) and remains the view expounded by Peter Comestor in his *Historia scholastica*, chap. 9 (PL 198:1063–64).

27. Fol. 7r of the Cotton Genesis illustrated the J-text Creation with two miniatures, an upper one with the *Forming of Adam*, and a lower one with both the *Enlivenment of Adam* and the *Animation of Adam*, while fol. 5v illustrated Gen. 1:26–27. Weitzmann and Kessler, 52–53 and 129–30, also state that the presence of the psyche figure in the Cotton Genesis is "virtually certain." Regarding the Cotton Genesis's use of an early Christian three-part Creation and the dualist model of the later Middle Ages used at San Marco, see U. Schubert, "Eine jüdische Vor-lage für die Darstellung der Erschaffung des Menschen in der sogen-annten Cotton-Genesis-Rezension?" in *Atti del IX Congresso interna-zionale di archeologia cristiana, Rome, 1975*, 2 vols., Vatican City, 1978, 1:433–49.

28. Weitzmann and Kessler, *The Cotton Genesis*, 53, offer no reason for their suggestion that the first tree is "presumably the tree of knowledge of good and evil."

29. Weitzmann, in Demus, *Mosaics of San Marco*, 2:113, doubts that the personifications appeared in the Cotton Genesis because of the "un-classical manner" in which all four point "upward" and because they appear in no other members of the Cotton Genesis family. He admits the possibility of their inclusion, although he believes they would have been passive rather than active. Weitzmann also notes the probable conflation at San Marco of what were two scenes in the model, the *In-troduction* and the *Admonition*. Consult also Weitzmann and Kessler, 53.

30. See Demus, *Mosaics of San Marco*, 2:78, regarding the original mosaic inscription, which is reset and probably in altered form today. Weitz-mann (in Demus, *Mosaics of San Marco*, 2:113) bases his opinion on the text of the inscription, but this seems to be an error, for in either

form—as Demus corrects it or as it currently reads—the inscription is an edited version of Gen. 2:9, where the two trees are first mentioned just after Adam's arrival in Eden. Neither version specifically includes the admonitory text of Gen. 2:16–17. It is my belief that it is not the verbal text that confirms the reference to admonition, but rather the left-handed gestures. If God's left-handed gesture here does not indicate speech, then his command in Gen. 2:16–17 is one of only two divine speeches from Gen. 1–3 that are omitted at San Marco. The other is Gen. 1:29–30, a speech that lies between the first and second Creations and thus was logically omitted in the "splicing" of the P- and J-text Creations.

Chapter Three

1. Bertoli, *I mosaici di San Marco*, 70, discusses the prominence of the lion, also honored in the following Noah scenes.

2. Weitzmann and Kessler, *The Cotton Genesis*, 54, point out that in the model, God originally stood to the picture's far left, Adam to its right, and the animals in the middle.

3. Evans, *"Paradise Lost" and the Genesis Traditions*, 39–40, discusses these rabbinical texts.

4. Chaps. 9 and 16 (PL 198:1063–64 and 1069–70); and see Evans's discussion of the text, 168–72.

5. O. Demus, *Byzantine Mosaic Decoration*, New Rochelle, N.Y., 1948, 8, discusses this Byzantine tradition, which would have been known in thirteenth-century Venice, as does Camille, *The Gothic Idol*, 223. Generally, evil figures were placed in profile so that the viewer could not be "trapped" by gazing into their eyes.

6. As in the approximately contemporary sculpture of the standing Christ by Nicola and Giovanni Pisano (Siena Cathedral Pulpit of 1265–68) or the thirteenth-century *Bible moralisée* illustrations, which contrast Eve's creation and her marriage to Adam to those of Ecclesia. See G. Schiller, *Iconography of Christian Art*, trans. J. Seligman, 2 vols., Greenwich, Conn., 1971, 2:134, 153, and fig. 507, and L. Silver and S. Smith, "Carnal Knowledge: The Late Engravings of Lucas van Leyden," *Nederlands Kunsthistorisch Jaarboek* 29 (1978): 259 and n. 82. That the taking of Adam's rib prophesies Christ's union with Ecclesia is standard, for example, in Peter Comestor's *Historia scholastica* and in Thomas Aquinas's *Summa theologica* of c. 1266–72 (pt. I, q. 92, arts. 2 and 3).

7. On Christ's wound, see Friedman, "More on 'Right' and 'Left' in Painting," 124 and 129–30, and V. Gurewich, "Observations on the

Iconography of the Wound in Christ's Side, with Special Reference to Its Position," *Journal of the Warburg and Courtauld Institutes* 20 (1957): 358–62. The associations of right (dexter) with positive traits and left (sinister) with evil ones are pervasive by the thirteenth century. Long-standing traditions were established in the ancient world, for example, the Greeks seeing the right as auspicious, and the left as ill-fortuned (C. J. Fordyce, *Catullus*, Oxford, 1961, 205–6; I thank Leslie Mechem for this reference). At the same time, medical discussions of the origins of the male and female linked male fetuses to those produced by sperm from the right testicle and eggs that implanted on the right side of the uterus, and females with those from and on the left. While Aristotle doubts the accuracy of this theory, it is repeated by many writers, from Galen (second cent.) to Albertus Magnus (twelfth cent.) to Levinus Lemnius (sixteenth cent.), and only seriously challenged beginning c. 1600. Thus the "leftness" of females is associated with their various physical and spiritual deficiencies. See H. R. Lemay, "Some Thirteenth- and Fourteenth-Century Lectures on Female Sexuality," *International Journal of Women's Studies* 1 (1978): 391–400, who demonstrates how theological views of women merged with medical ones, leading to assertions that women's biological inferiority was dangerous to men; J. Cadden, *Meanings of Sex Difference in the Middle Ages: Medicine, Science, and Culture*, Cambridge and New York, 1993, 130–34; and I. Maclean, *The Renaissance Notion of Woman*, Cambridge, 1980, chap. 3, especially 37–44, and 87–88, who includes many other medical stereo-types concerning the female body, e.g., as a privative version of the male, as naturally passive.

Various of the Kabbalah texts, many of which were being written in the thirteenth century, also examine the qualities of "right" and "left." See G. Scholem, *Kabbalah*, Jerusalem, 1974, 117 and 123, where left is associated with the power of uncleanliness and evil, active in Creation, and Bamberger, *Fallen Angels*, 173–86. J. Schuyler ("The Left Side of God: A Reflection of Cabala in Michelangelo's Genesis Scenes," *Source* 6 [1986]: 12–19) writes about the significance of the left-sided creation of Eve in Michelangelo's Sistine Ceiling, linking it there to inferior feminine principles of the left side of the Sefiroth discussed in the Kab-balah. Muslim tradition relates that Eve was created from Adam's left side (*The Jewish Encyclopedia*, New York and London, 1901–6, 5:275). Probably several of these medical and theological traditions contrib-uted to Eve's creation from Adam's left side here at San Marco, all of which reconfirm her inherent inferiority.

8.   The first-century writer Philo notes this, as does John Scotus Erigena (ninth cent.), who understood the Fall as occurring during Adam's sleep (Evans, *"Paradise Lost" and the Genesis Traditions*, 72 and 77).

Innocent III (Lothario dei Segni, d. 1216), in his *De miseria humanae conditionis*, confirms that "in carnal intercourse the mind's clarity is put to sleep" (ed. D. R. Howard, trans. M. M. Dietz, Indianapolis and New York, 1969, 8).

9. Weitzmann and Kessler, *The Cotton Genesis*, 54, note that some early Christian commentators made a connection between Adam's trance at Eve's birth and drunkenness. Noah's drunkenness is also a type for the Passion of Christ. Weitzmann and Kessler reconstruct the Cotton Genesis miniature with God first in the scene, followed by Adam; thus San Marco's mosaicists have reversed the figures.

10. Honorius of Autun, in his *De imagine mundi* of c. 1154–59, affirms that it was the wood of the Tree of Knowledge that was planted in Adam's mouth at Calvary. See J. O'Reilly, *Studies in the Iconography of the Virtues and Vices*, Ph.D. diss., University of Nottingham, 1972; Garland Reprint, New York, 1988, 342. Jacopo da Voragine's thirteenth-century *Golden Legend*, in the entry for May 3 ("Invention of the Holy Cross"), includes several versions of the story involving a tree of mercy—it is unclear which tree that is—and one where a branch from the tree that "caused Adam to sin" was planted in his mouth by Seth and became the tree of the Cross (ed. G. Ryan and H. Ripperger, New York, 1969, 269–70). Schiller, *Iconography of Christian Art*, 2:12–14 and 130–34, recounts a number of the legends linking Adam to the Tree of Life and the Cross, as does O'Reilly, 341–48. Both confirm the popularity of tree legends in the twelfth and thirteenth centuries, partly due to Franciscan interest in the Cross (Bonaventura, for example, writes his meditations on the Cross) and partly due to the proliferation of relics of the True Cross in Europe at the time of the Crusades. San Marco itself housed an important relic of the True Cross in its Treasury, as will be discussed below.

11. There are numerous such crosses and trees, e.g., Schiller, 2:130–33, where figs. 15, 339, 389, 478, and 479 illustrate the former type, and figs. 370, 373, and 480 the latter (examples all date from the tenth to the thirteenth centuries). She also illustrates other traditions of Adam (and sometimes Eve) at the base of the Cross, e.g., where the tree or Cross grows from Adam's head, or where Adam squats like a telamon, supporting the Cross.

12. Bal, "Sexuality, Sin, and Sorrow," 323, discusses these terms, as does Bloom, *The Book of J*, 175–76 and 179–80. Analysis of this language and other parts of the Genesis text has led a number of contemporary biblical scholars to propose that the Genesis text per se is not particularly antifemale, but that later exegesis established the misogynist readings. Trible was one of the first to postulate this; more recently, Bloom has hypothesized that the J text was intended to be read ironically. Cer-

tainly the San Marco mosaics qualify as a misogynist *rewriting* of Genesis.

13. As Joan Cadden notes, there is no single, widely held view regarding the differences between Adam and Eve in European culture between the late eleventh and fourteenth centuries, yet all writers find difference. See her *Meanings of Sex Difference in the Middle Ages,* 2 and passim. Particularly useful is her chap. 3, "Academic Questions: Female and Male in Scholastic Medicine and Natural Philosophy."

14. On this mind-body duality of Adam and Eve, and Eve's association with the sensual, see P. Allen, *The Concept of Woman: The Aristotelian Revolution, 750 B.C.–A.D. 1250,* Montreal and London, 1985, passim, who summarizes succinctly Augustine's complexly contradictory views regarding males and females (218–36); A. K. Hieatt, "Eve as Reason in a Tradition of Allegorical Interpretations of the Fall," *Journal of the Warburg and Courtauld Institutes* 43 (1980): 221–26; Ruether, "Misogynism and Virginal Feminism," 150–83; and E. Pagels, *Adam, Eve, and the Serpent,* New York, 1988, 64–65, 113–14, and passim.

15. M. M. McLaughlin, "Peter Abelard and the Dignity of Women: Twelfth-Century 'Feminism' in Theory and Practice," in *Pierre Abélard, Pierre le Vénérable. Les courants philosophiques, littéraires et artistiques en occident au milieu du XIIe siècle (Colloques internationaux du Centre national de la recherche scientifique, Cluny, 1972),* Paris, 1975, 306; and Allen, *The Concept of Woman,* 271–92.

16. E. C. McLaughlin, "Equality of Souls, Inequality of Sexes: Woman in Medieval Theology," in *Religion and Sexism,* ed. R. R. Ruether, New York, 1974, 217–19. In addition to summarizing Aquinas's views on males and females, Allen (*The Concept of Woman,* 385–407) treats a number of other important writers of the later Middle Ages, including Hildegard of Bingen and Albertus Magnus.

17. Brunetto Latino, in his *Livres dou tresor,* quoted in the unsigned introduction to *Equally in God's Image,* ed. J. B. Holloway, C. S. Wright, and J. Bechtold, New York, 1990, 4.

18. See below the discussion of *Eve Plucking the Fruit and Tempting Adam* regarding the common interpretation that Eve seduced Adam.

19. Demus, *Mosaics of San Marco,* 1:4, 66, and 244 n. 323. A commemorative mosaic was added over the Treasury door in c. 1235 (see Demus, 2:56 and pl. 101). D. Pincus, "Christian Relics and the Body Politic: A Thirteenth-Century Relief Plaque in the Church of San Marco," in *Interpretazioni veneziane. Studi di storia dell'arte in onore di Michelangelo Muraro,* ed. D. Rosand, Venice, 1984, 39–57, discusses the circumstances surrounding the fire and subsequent miracle.

20. Tree of Jesse images were widespread by the mid-twelfth century in Europe and drew on the popular association between the Latin *virgo* and

virga. See, for example, Schiller, *Iconography of Christian Art,* 1 : 15 − 22, and O'Reilly, *Studies in the Iconography of the Virtues and Vices,* 359 − 61.

21. A. Katzenellenbogen, *Allegories of the Virtues and Vices in Medieval Art,* New York, 1964, 63 – 68, discusses these, as does O'Reilly in her chap. 8. Attention to this theme at San Marco is further evidenced by the addition to its facade of reliefs of the Virtues in the thirteenth century (Demus, *Mosaics of San Marco,* 1 : 267).

22. J. Beck, "Genesis, Sexual Antagonism, and the Defective Couple of the Twelfth-Century *Jeu d'Adam,*" *Representations* 29 (1990): 124 and 128, has an interesting discussion of similar reversals of cause and effect in the *Jeu d'Adam,* a twelfth-century religious play of the Fall.

23. Schreiner, "Eve, the Mother of History," 142 – 47, discusses this section of *De Genesi ad litteram.* Augustine insists that the souls were not gendered until given bodies in Gen. 2, implying an equality, yet, as noted above, his discussion of the male and female souls clearly identifies Eve's as inferior.

24. D. Markow, "The Iconography of the Soul in Medieval Art," Ph.D. diss., New York University, 1985, 34 – 42, in an intelligent and persuasive discussion of this group of cycles, reidentifies the scene, noting that earlier scholars had sometimes misidentified these as the Separation of Light and Darkness of Day One of Creation. The group includes six Western church cycles (the nave frescoes at San Paolo fuori le mura, Rome, c. 700, known through seventeenth-century drawings [Fig. 17]; frescoes in the Lateran Palace, Rome, first quarter twelfth century; frescoes at San Pietro in Ferentillo from the late twelfth century; at San Giovanni a Porta Latina from 1191 – 98; mosaics in the Baptistry, Florence, probably produced during the 1270s [Plate 10]; and the upper nave wall frescoes attributed to Jacopo Torriti in the Upper Church of San Francesco, Assisi, ca. 1290 [Plate 9]), two Umbrian-Roman illustrated twelfth-century Bibles (Vat. pal. lat. 3, fol. 5, and Perugia, Communale L. 59), and a thirteenth-century processional cross (San Giovanni Laterano, Treasury).

25. The three other frescoes that show her turning away include those at the Lateran Palace, at Assisi (Plate 9), and at San Giovanni a Porta Latina.

26. *Summa theologica* pt. I, q. 92. Questions regarding the nature and acquisition of Eve's soul relative to animals' and to Adam's souls were discussed by many medieval theologians. According to some, because Adam's flesh was already animate when his rib was removed, Eve had a rational soul from her first moment, but, as noted above in chap. 3 n. 14, it was judged inferior to Adam's.

27. See pt. I, q. 92 of Aquinas's *Summa theologica* and the discussion of it in E. C. McLaughlin, "Equality of Souls, Inequality of Sexes," especially

217–19. Maclean, *The Renaissance Notion of Woman*, 3, discusses Aristotle's four categories of contraries relative to medieval and renaissance understandings of male and female. In many instances, from legal writings to medical texts, females were understood to be deprived (and therefore defective) versions of the male, as darkness is a state of being deprived of light.

28. D. Wolfthal, "'A Hue and a Cry': Medieval Rape Imagery and Its Transformation," *Art Bulletin* 75 (1993): 41–42, discusses the gesture of wrist holding as one of force and control. God similarly holds Adam during the scene of the forming and when he introduces him into Eden.

29. *Summa theologica* pt. 1, q. 92, art. 2.

30. Schreiner, "Eve, the Mother of History," 155, so paraphrases Augustine. Leo Steinberg offers his most recent views on Michelangelo's hand gesture for Eve in "The Line of Fate," *Critical Inquiry* 6 (1980): 439–43. He suggests that Eve's stiff middle finger, which points at her own pudendum, designates her "receptive womb" (440), and he links this to her concupiscence with Adam, her future motherhood, and the role of woman's womb in salvation. The "finger addresses that port of sin which, by grace of that other Eve, becomes the gate of redemption" (441). Augustine, posing the question of why Eve was created, reasons in the following way in *De Genesi ad litteram* 9.5.9 (quoted and discussed in Schreiner, 153): certainly she was not there to help him till the soil, since a male would be far preferable; similarly, she was not as "agreeable for companionship and conversation" as a male would be. Thus, he concludes, she is there "as a helper in begetting children." Schreiner, 155–59, summarizes Augustine's view of the origins of human and angelic history.

31. Beck discusses similar ideas in his analysis of the *Jeu d'Adam*.

Chapter Four

1. Ancient and medieval medical texts, influenced by Aristotle and Galen, emphasize this difference between the male's naturally active nature and the female's natural passivity. See Maclean's chap. 3 ("Medicine, Anatomy, Physiology," in his *Renaissance Notion of Woman*), especially 30 and 44. The active-passive dichotomy is repeated by many medieval theologians.

2. Weitzmann and Kessler, *The Cotton Genesis*, 55. Examples of texts that have both Adam and Eve present at the admonition include the *Vita Adae et Evae* (ed. J. H. Charlesworth, *The Old Testament Pseudepigrapha*, 2 vols., Garden City, N.Y., 1985, 2:270, 271, and 279) and the twelfth-

century mystery play, the *Jeu d'Adam* (ll. 101–4 in *Adam, a Religious Play of the Twelfth Century*, trans. E. N. Stone, Seattle, 1928, 162–63). See also J. M. Higgins, "The Myth of Eve: The Temptress," *Journal of the American Academy of Religion* 44 (1976): 645–47.

3. Tertullian, in his "Of the Flesh of Christ," chap. 17 (*The Ante-Nicene Christian Library*, ed. A. Roberts and J. Donaldson, 24 vols., Edinburgh, 1868–72, 15:200–201), is one of the first to suggest that Eve's conversation with the Serpent was a type for the Annunciation and notes the importance of believing words for both. The two scenes are standardly paired in the late-thirteenth-century *Biblia pauperum* (see A. Henry, *Biblia Pauperum*, Ithaca, N.Y., 1987), and many textual accounts of the Fall stress the role of ears and speech, e.g., the *Jeu d'Adam* (e.g., ll. 205–42, 465–68, and stage directions following l. 292) and the *Vita Adae et Evae* (Charlesworth, *The Old Testament Pseudepigrapha*, 2:277–81).

4. Although the Genesis text makes no reference to the identity of or source for the Serpent, early exegesis and popular legends identified him either as Lucifer (i.e., Satan, the Devil) or as the mouthpiece for Lucifer. See J. B. Russell, *Satan: The Early Christian Tradition*, Ithaca, N.Y., and London, 1981, 66–67, 78–79, and 82; and Bamberger, *Fallen Angels*, passim. In the *Vita Adae et Evae*, for example, the Devil says to the Serpent, "Do not fear; only become my vessel, and I will speak a word through your mouth by which you will be able to deceive him" (Charlesworth, *The Old Testament Pseudepigrapha*, 2:277). Peter Comestor explains that God does not question the Serpent following the Fall, because his actions were really the Devil's (chap. 23, PL 198:1073).

5. *The Cotton Genesis*, 55. Their fig. 42 shows the remaining right half of the Cotton Genesis miniature with Eve and the Serpent in the tree; the left side is lost.

6. *Historia scholastica*, chap. 21 (PL 198:1072). In the same chapter, Comestor describes Adam as upright (*erectus*). William Caxton's translation is at the very opening of his edition of the *Golden Legend* (*The Golden Legend or Lives of the Saints as Englished by William Caxton*, 7 vols., London, 1922, 1:173).

7. Ibid.

8. The Genesis text does not specify the type of fruit eaten, saying only that Adam and Eve later cover themselves with fig leaves (Gen. 3:7), but the *Vita Adae et Evae* states that Eve ate the fruit of the fig (Charlesworth, *The Old Testament Pseudepigrapha*, 2:281). In that account, the Serpent bends over the wall of Paradise when persuading Eve to eat, and she opens the gate to him and follows him "a little" before they come to the Tree of Knowledge (ibid., 2:279).

9. Augustine helped establish the tradition that the Tree of Knowledge

was inherently good, but the first parents' act of disobedience, evil. For his and some other views, consult Evans, *"Paradise Lost" and the Genesis Traditions*, 79, 89, and 96.

10. Bal, "Sexuality, Sin, and Sorrow," 328, and Higgins, "The Myth of Eve," 645–46, discuss the Hebrew text; Flavius Josephus, *Antiquities of the Jews* 1:1, in *The Works of Flavius Josephus*, trans. W. Whiston, Hartford, Conn., 1919, has the Serpent speak to them both.

11. The question of why Adam sinned and whether or not he was deceived by Eve has been discussed by numerous medieval writers. See chap. 4 nn. 18–19 below.

12. Weitzmann and Kessler, *The Cotton Genesis*, 55, believe that the figure of Adam is a remnant of the missing admonition scene, but there is no reason for Adam to speak there, either.

13. R. Mellinkoff, "Riding Backwards: Theme of Humiliation and Symbol of Evil," *Viator* 4 (1973): 153–76, discusses the functions of "backwardness" in both society and art in her discussion of equestrian riders, linking such reversed figures to folly, humiliation, and evil.

14. Bal, "Sexuality, Sin, and Sorrow," 327–28. See the further discussion of the "HIC" texts below in chap. 6.

15. In the *Introduction of Eve to Adam*, she stands alongside the Creator but is passive and does not raise her right hand. She also partially parallels the Lord and Adam in the *Expulsion* but, unlike either of them, turns her head back and gestures with her left hand.

16. The *Vita Adae et Evae*, a text that may be a source for these mosaics, explains that as soon as Eve ate, "at that very moment my eyes were opened and I [Eve] knew that I was naked of the righteousness with which I had been clothed." Only because she had sworn an oath to the Serpent that she would also feed Adam, did she then speak to and tempt Adam, but it was the Devil who was speaking through her (Charlesworth, *The Old Testament Pseudepigrapha*, 2:281).

17. See chap. 3 n. 5 above.

18. Higgins, "The Myth of Eve," 642–44, summarizes varied explanations for why Adam sinned, as does Evans, *"Paradise Lost" and the Genesis Traditions*, passim.

19. For example, Peter Comestor (PL 198:1072) and Rupert of Deutz both credit Eve's persuasiveness to speech (Higgins, "The Myth of Eve," 642–44), and the former is responsible for the wide popularity of this explanation. Augustine (*De Genesi ad litteram* 11.30) had also suggested that Eve might have been persuasive with words. Others explained Eve's power as one of sexual seduction, even though the Vulgate text makes no such suggestion. See B. P. Prusak, "Woman: Seductive Siren and Source of Sin? Pseudepigraphal Myth and Christian Origins," in *Religion and Sexism*, ed. R. R. Ruether, New York,

1974, 89–116; and Higgins, passim, who points out that the Genesis text never even specifies that Eve was in any way coercive (Gen. 3:6: "and she took of the fruit thereof, and did eat, and gave to her husband who did eat"). The *Vita Adae et Evae* stresses Eve's verbal cogency: "[The Serpent] sprinkled his evil poison on the fruit which he gave me to eat which is his covetousness," and then "I [Eve] spoke to him [Adam] unlawful words of transgression. . . . For when he came, I opened my mouth and the devil was speaking, and I began to admonish him" (Charlesworth, *The Old Testament Pseudepigrapha*, 2:279 and 281). Both of these powers—beguiling words and carnal seduction—became associated with the power of women in general.

20. Eve's first speech is in reply to the Serpent's question ("cui respondit mulier"; Gen. 3:2) and the second in reply to God's question ("quae respondit"; Gen. 3:13). Never given the *dixit* or *ait* formulas—although the Serpent, Adam, and God all use them—she initiates speech when she bears and names Cain (Gen. 4:1; see the discussion of *The Birth of Cain* below) and Seth (Gen. 5:25). Pardes, *Countertraditions*, 49–51, discusses Eve's role in those texts, and more generally the name-bestowing role of females in the Old Testament. As she notes, when Adam "births" Eve and names her, there is a sex-role reversal. Bal, "Sexuality, Sin, and Sorrow," 320–22 and passim, discusses the significance of having a name, for many Old Testament women remain nameless. Eve remarkably receives two names in the Genesis text, both given her by Adam: "Woman" (Gen. 2:23; immediately following her forming) and "Eve" (Gen. 3:20; immediately following God's curses on them, prior to their being clothed). Bal also discusses speech as a device of characterization. Her ideas on naming and characterization are expanded in her *Lethal Love: Feminist Literary Readings of Biblical Love Stories*, Bloomington and Indianapolis, 1987, especially chap. 3.

21. Both M. Pellegrino, "Il 'topos' della 'status rectus' nel contesto filosofico e biblico," in *Mullus, Festschrift Theodor Klauser*, vol. 1 of *Jahrbuch für Antike und Christentum*, Münster, 1964, 273–81, and O. K. Werckmeister, "The Lintel Fragment Representing Eve from Saint-Lazare, Autun," *Journal of the Warburg and Courtauld Institutes* 35 (1972): 23–27, discuss the meaning of erect and bent postures. The association of upright postures with moral righteousness and twisted ones with moral depravity is a commonplace in medieval writings about human souls or the Virtues and Vices. For example, Augustine (*City of God* 14.11) writes that "God . . . made man upright, and consequently with a good will" (trans. Dods, 457).

22. Comestor, *Historia scholastica*, chap. 23 (PL 198:1073). See Evans's explication of Comestor's text, especially 171–72 and 178, in *"Paradise Lost" and the Genesis Traditions*.

23. Weitzmann and Kessler, *The Cotton Genesis*, 56, believe that the Cotton Genesis did include the Serpent, because it appears in several other works in the recension.

24. Once again there are similarities between the mosaics and the several versions of the narrative generally referred to as the *Vita Adae et Evae*. There, from the very beginning of the accounts, Eve accepts blame for the Fall, even offering to die if that would allow Adam to return to Eden (Charlesworth, *The Old Testament Pseudepigrapha*, 2:258 and 259).

25. The fact that the Deity needed to ask questions of Adam and Eve might seem to demonstrate a failure in his omniscience and is one of the distinguishing features of the J text.

26. Charlesworth, *The Old Testament Pseudepigrapha*, 2:281.

27. Also noted by Weitzmann, in Demus, *Mosaics of San Marco*, 2:115.

28. See M. Bernabò, "La cacciata dal Paradiso e il lavoro dei progenitori in alcune miniature medievali," in *Congresso di storia della miniatura italiana. Atti del I Congresso, Cortona, 1978. La miniatura italiana in età romanica e gotica*, Florence, 1979, 276−77; similarly, Comestor sees the coats of skins as signs of human mortality. For Ambrose's ideas that clothing functions as a mark of sin, and Luther's that it reminded Adam and Eve of their sin, consult M. R. Miles, *Carnal Knowing: Female Nakedness and Religious Meaning in the Christian West*, Boston, 1989, 92−93 and 109, who also discusses other aspects of clothing. The concept of clothing in medieval Europe is complex and ambiguous. On the one hand, clothing represents civilization and order, and carries information regarding status and power; on the other, its origins were associated with sin and loss of perfection. E. Kosmer, "The 'noyous humoure of lecherie,'" *Art Bulletin* 57 (1975): 5−6, discusses additional Christian ideas regarding clothing and nudity, as does J. Z. Smith, "The Garments of Shame," *History of Religions* 5 (1966): 217−38.

29. The discrepancy regarding the length of Eve's dress is noted by Weitzmann, in Demus, *Mosaics of San Marco*, 2:116. Aschkenasy, *Eve's Journey*, 52−53, discusses exposed legs and feet, noting that the Hebrew term *regel* (leg or foot) was a euphemism for intercourse. J. Williams, "*Generationes Abrahae:* Reconquest Iconography in Leon," *Gesta* 16 (1977): 8−9, discusses the provocative action of lifting one's skirt and baring a leg.

30. On the phoenix, see H. L. Kessler, "The Solitary Bird in van der Goes' Garden of Eden," *Journal of the Warburg and Courtauld Institutes* 28 (1965): 326−29, who notes that a variety of traditions existed concerning the color of phoenixes, and Weitzmann and Kessler, *The Cotton Genesis*, 58.

31. Weitzmann and Kessler, 57, and Weitzmann, in Demus, *Mosaics of San Marco*, 2:116.

32. Charlesworth, *The Old Testament Pseudepigrapha*, 2:285.

33. M. Barasch, *Gestures of Despair in Medieval and Early Renaissance Art*,
    New York, 1976, 13–14, examines similarities between Expulsions of
    Adam and Eve and the damned in Hell. The *Jeu d'Adam* (trans. Stone,
    178) has Adam and Eve laboring and lamenting their fate, when several
    devils enter and shackle them, pushing them into Hell.

Chapter Five

1. The topos of a text or image functioning as a *speculum*—mirror—is
   found repeatedly in thirteenth- and fourteenth-century Europe. Mirrors were typically round at that time, so cupolas carry a particular at-
   traction for this sort of comparison. Overviews of mirror symbolism
   are found in G. F. Hartlaub, *Zauber des Spiegels. Geschichte und Bedeu-
   tung des Spiegels in der Kunst*, Munich, 1951; H. Schwarz, "The Mirror
   in Art," *Art Quarterly* 15 (1959): 96–118; and a special double issue of
   Source (5, Winter–Spring 1985), which contains articles devoted entirely to mirrors, with updated bibliographies. Particularly relevant to
   this study are R. Baldwin's "Plutarch's Wife as Mirror in a German Renaissance Marriage Portrait" (68–71) and N. Salomon's "A Woman's
   Place: The Queen in *Las Meninas*" (72–79). Salomon discusses the reversal of the queen's and king's normal positions, the queen appearing
   at the picture's privileged right and the king at its left.

2. Elsewhere in the Bible spinning is associated with the good wife and
   women in general, e.g., Exod. 35:25–26 and Prov. 31:19. Echoing
   other medieval authors, Geoffrey Chaucer, writing the "Prologue to
   the Wife of Bath's Tale" for his *Canterbury Tales* about a century later
   than the mosaics, sees spinning as natural to women: "Deceite, wepyng,
   spynnyng God hath yive / To wommen kyndely, whil that they may
   lyve" (ll. 401–2). Some useful ideas and bibliography on spinning are
   found in L. F. Hodges, "Noe's Wife: Type of Eve and Wakefield Spinner," in *Equally in God's Image*, ed. J. B. Holloway, C. S. Wright, and
   J. Bechtold, New York, 1990, 30–39. Scholars have been unable to as-
   certain a specific textual source for Eve's use of a spindle and distaff,
   although H. L. Kessler, *The Illustrated Bibles from Tours*, Princeton,
   1977, 22, quotes a Syrian commentary on Genesis, where God "in-
   structed the woman (Eve) in the art of weaving." See in the text below
   a quotation from Tertullian, which may also be relevant. Eve is associated with cloth making and Adam with agriculture at least as early as
   the fourth-century sarcophagus of Junius Bassus, where she is shown
   with a sheep and Adam with a sheaf of wheat. Interestingly, that Eve
   spun during her labors is specified in the *Speculum humanae salvationis*
   (first quarter fourteenth cent.), but its unknown author must have been

unaware of any legitimate textual source, for he cites a false reference to Gen. 7 (in J. Lutz and P. Perdrizet, *Speculum humanae salvationis. Traduction inédite de Jean Miélot [1448]*, 2 vols., Leipzig, 1907, 2:185. These authors link the tradition to a verse popular in the Middle Ages: "Quand Adam bechait, quand Eve filait / Où donc était le gentilhomme?").

3. P. Molmenti, *Venice: Its Individual Growth from the Earliest Beginnings to the Fall of the Republic*, pt. 1, *The Middle Ages*, 2 vols., Bergamo, 1906, 2:42, notes this in the *statuti* of Chioggia of both 1272 and 1291. Because Creation took six days, and on the seventh day God rested, the eighth day was associated with the start of the earthly realm of work. Perhaps this demarcated the end of the "honeymoon"?

4. Weitzmann and Kessler, *The Cotton Genesis*, 37–38, and Weitzmann, in Demus, *Mosaics of San Marco*, 2:116, where he adds that it is possible that the Cotton Genesis included the spindle and distaff, but that the throne was very unlikely. Regarding Eve and Mary, see the classic treatment in E. Guldan, *Eva und Maria*, Graz and Cologne, 1966, and the recent and very useful exhibition catalogue by H. D. Russell, *Eva/ Ave: Woman in Renaissance and Baroque Prints*, Washington and New York, 1990, especially 113–39. Demus, *Mosaics of San Marco*, 1:41, notes that this is a Western, not Byzantine, typology.

5. This last forms the southern vestibule through which one can enter the atrium, directly below the cupola of the Creation; see Demus, *Mosaics of San Marco*, 1:40–41. For the other churches, see Borsook, *Messages in Mosaic*, 62, and Schiller, *Iconography of Christian Art*, 1:37.

6. S. Sinding-Larsen, *Christ in the Council Hall: Studies in the Religious Iconography of the Venetian Republic*, Rome, 1974, 203, on Venice's founding. There are many examples of a seated Eve at the scene of the labors, sometimes with and sometimes without a distaff and/or spindle, but most commonly the reference is to her role as mother of all living (Gen. 3:20), for she generally sits and nurses one or more children. The San Marco mosaic is unusual in its combination of an enthroned Eve (not just seated on a hillock), with distaff and spindles, dressed in greater finery than Adam, *and* without children. That she is not pregnant yet is indicated by the scene of Cain's conception, which follows in the lunette below, an event that was understood to represent Adam and Eve's first postlapsarian carnal encounter.

7. E. Hennecke, *New Testament Apocrypha*, ed. W. Schneemelcher, trans. R. Wilson, 2 vols., Philadelphia, 1963, 1:379–80. G. M. Gibson discusses this text and iconographic motif in "The Thread of Life in the Hand of the Virgin," in *Equally in God's Image*, ed. J. B. Holloway, C. S. Wright, and J. Bechtold, New York, 1990, 46–54. Eve as an antitype for Mary is also found at San Marco in the *Temptation of Eve* (see discussion above).

8. A recent examination of the Santa Maria Maggiore *Annunciation* appears in J. Sieger, "Visual Metaphor as Theology: Leo the Great's Sermons on the Incarnation and the Arch Mosaics at S. Maria Maggiore," *Gesta* 26 (1987): 85–86. In a Byzantine-inspired, ninth-century ivory from Charlemagne's court, Mary wears military garb and sits with spindles and cross-scepter; consult S. Lewis, "A Byzantine 'Virgo militans' at Charlemagne's Court," *Viator* 11 (1980): 71–93, especially 73–75, on the relationship of spindles to the Incarnation. An example that is closer chronologically is at Monreale: the late-twelfth-century *Annunciation*, in front of the apse and directly opposite Eve on the west wall, shows Mary standing with distaff in hand. See Borsook, *Messages in Mosaic*, 62 and pls. 62 and 86; pl. 88 shows Eve seated at her labors with a distaff.

9. Exegesis differs on this point. Some understood Gen. 3:22 to mean that Adam was not immortal prior to the Fall but could become immortal were he to eat of the Tree of Life. See Bloom, *The Book of J*, 186.

10. *The Antiquities of the Jews* 1.1.

11. See S. L. Smith, "The Power of Women *Topos* on a Fourteenth-Century Embroidery," *Viator* 21 (1990): 212–13, regarding Adam's bestial nature following the Fall, where she paraphrases Thomas of Cîteaux and quotes John of Salisbury (the English translation is mine). While it is unlikely that the Venetian mosaicists knew these specific texts, they are representative of the Middle Ages. Pellegrino ("Il 'topos' della 'status rectus'") discusses this pre-Christian and Christian idea of humans' differing from animals due to reason; this was expressed visually through their *status erectus*.

12. The question of who sinned more terribly was considered carefully by medieval exegetes. Typically, their conclusions are complex, on the one hand stressing that because Adam was more perfect, he fell farther, yet also noting that Eve sinned twice as much. Not only did she disobey God, but she also led Adam astray. Evans, *"Paradise Lost" and the Genesis Traditions*, especially 178–82, reviews this issue of relative guilt according to a variety of medieval authors.

13. Augustine examines this issue in several of his writings, for example, *The City of God* 14.23 and *De Genesis ad litteram* 9.4 (Evans, 94, examines Augustine's position).

14. Barr, "The Influence of St. Jerome on Medieval Attitudes to Women," 94–95, and idem, "The Vulgate Genesis," 127, compares the Hebrew version of Gen. 3:16 ("Your desire will be for your husband, and he will rule over you") to Jerome's Vulgate ("You will be under the power of your husband, and he will rule over you"). She confirms that the Old Latin version retained the older sexual meaning. The Cotton Genesis was a Greek translation of the Old Latin text, not the Vulgate. Pagels,

Adam, Eve, and the Serpent, chap. 6, passim, discusses Augustinian and other early perspectives on the punishments of Adam and Eve, including that of "desire."

15. On this theme in general, see S. L. Smith, "'To Women's Wiles I Fell': The Power of Women *Topos* and the Development of Medieval Secular Art," Ph.D. diss., University of Pennsylvania, 1978, passim; idem, *The Power of Women*, Philadelphia, 1995, passim; Silver and Smith, "Carnal Knowledge: The Late Engravings of Lucas van Leyden," especially 250–57, where they suggest that the earliest Fall used as an example of the Power of Women is found in the early-fourteenth-century Distaff House in Constance. Smith, "'To Women's Wiles I Fell,'" 273–77, discusses these murals further, and on 44 notes that it was St. Jerome who first identified Adam as a victim in the Power of Women theme. The distaff here then functions as a mock scepter for Eve but also derides Adam: distaffs were sometimes attributes of the cuckold. See Camille, *The Gothic Idol*, 301–2, and A. G. Stewart, *Unequal Lovers: A Study of Unequal Couples in Northern Art*, New York, 1979.

16. See N. Z. Davis, *Society and Culture in Early Modern France*, Stanford, Calif., 1975, especially the chapters "The Reasons of Misrule" (97–123) and "Women on Top" (124–51) on the dynamics of this kind of imagery, which she calls "women on top." Others have argued that this kind of reversal only reasserts the orthodox hierarchy, but Davis disagrees, arguing (129) that the inversion could lead to new possibilities for women.

17. Ll. 255, 258, 445, and 447 (trans. Stone, 168 and 174).

18. Translation by this author of Jean Miélot's fifteenth-century French translation of the original Latin text: "et cellui qu'il vuelt estre laboureur aux champs, ne se doit vestir de soie" (Lutz and Perdrizet, *Speculum humanae salvationis*, 123). Chapter 1 of the *Speculum* text explains that Eve's first great sin was her proud wish to be like God; her second was to tempt Adam (Lutz and Perdrizet include both the original Latin fourteenth-century text, beginning on 4, and Miélot's, beginning on 122). Chapter 2 concerns Adam and Eve after the Expulsion and admonishes the reader to be wary of the deceitful and fraudulent world. Expressing many of the same ideas as the San Marco mosaics, the writer cautions that love of riches and fancy dress leads to damnation. The image illustrated here as Fig. 29 is from a Flemish manuscript of Miélot's text, illustrated c. 1485–95 and discussed in A. Wilson and J. L. Wilson, *A Medieval Mirror: Speculum humanae salvationis, 1324–1500*, Berkeley, Los Angeles, and London, 1984, 60–61.

19. See chap. 3 n. 21 above.

20. J. Alexander, "*Labeur* and *Paresse*: Ideological Representations of Medieval Peasant Labor," *Art Bulletin* 72 (1990): 447, discusses fourteenth-

and fifteenth-century examples of both peasants and Adam and Eve in fancy clothing as scenes of mockery and discusses this English illumination on 447. Already in the early Christian era avarice was sometimes associated with the Fall because some writers saw the Fall as greed for food, and this led to Adam's association with Dives. See P. Brown, *The Body and Society: Men, Women, and Sexual Renunciation in Early Christianity*, New York, 1988, 220 and 406. Several Middle Byzantine ivory caskets include a figure of Avarice or Wealth alongside the laboring Adam and Eve, and so may well refer to this ancient tradition. See, for example, the ivories illustrated in A. Goldschmidt and K. Weitzmann, *Die Byzantinischen Elfenbeinskulpturen des X.–XIII. Jahrhunderts*, 2d ed., vol. 5 of A. Goldschmidt, *Die Elfenbeinskulpturen*, Berlin, 1979, 1: nos. 68 and 69.

21. Chap. 21, "On Lust"; Dietz trans., 48.

22. See Williams's discussion of Hagar and Muslim women and their association with sexuality, in his *"Generationes Abrahae,"* as well as John Boswell's comments on thirteenth-century Europe's perception of Muslim sexual immorality in his *Christianity, Social Tolerance, and Homosexuality*, Chicago and London, 1980, 279–81. Potiphar's wife lived, of course, centuries before the establishment of Islam, but her actions caused her to be associated anachronistically with Muslims. The anti-Arab biases in the narthex mosaics at San Marco are also evident in the visual and textual narratives of Ishmael and Isaac. For example, Hagar is located to the picture's left when she gives birth to Ishmael, the privileged right being reserved for the standing figures of Abraham and Sarah (Demus, *Mosaics of San Marco*, 2: pl. 222), yet Sarah lies to the picture's right when she bears Isaac (2: colorpl. 50). At his circumcision Ishmael has his genitals exposed, a reference to his carnality, while in the immediately following *Circumcision of All Men* and later *Circumcision of Isaac*, no genitals are visible (2: pls. 226, 227, and 234). The choice and editing of the text in the Latin *tituli* for the Ishmael scenes reveal these same anti-Muslim prejudices. Venice's attitudes toward Egypt, specifically, were clearly complex in this age. Alexandria might have been "home" to St. Mark in the apostolic age, yet it was also the site of his martyrdom and the home of Arabs.

23. In this famous passage, Paul interweaves—in addition to pride, carnality, and submissiveness—two further themes recurrent at San Marco: the question of whether Eve was also made in God's image and the role of the fallen angels.

> But I want you to understand that the head of every man is Christ, the head of a woman is her husband, and the head of Christ is God. Any man who prays or prophesies with his head covered dishonors his head, but any woman who prays or prophesies with her head unveiled dishonors her head. . . . For a man ought not to cover his head, since he is the image and

> glory of God; but woman is the glory of man. (For man was not made from woman, but woman from man. Neither was man created for woman, but woman for man.) That is why a woman ought to have a veil on her head, because of the angels. . . . if a woman has long hair, it is her pride.

The "angels" is a reference to the legend of the Watcher Angels, who disrupted the divinely ordained hierarchy by falling victim to the seductive beauty of the daughters of men and defiling themselves with them sexually. For the legend of the Watcher Angels, which originates in Gen. 6:1–8, consult Prusak, "Woman: Seductive Siren and Source of Sin?" 90–93 and 98–104, and J. B. Russell, *The Devil: Perceptions of Evil from Antiquity to Primitive Christianity*, Ithaca, N.Y., and London, 1977, and idem, *Satan: The Early Christian Tradition* (indices, s.v. "Watcher Angels"). Several of the noncanonical Jewish texts relate (in varied forms) the story of the Watcher Angels, e.g., the Book of Jubilees 5 (R. H. Charles, ed., *The Apocrypha and Pseudepigrapha of the Old Testament in English*, 2 vols., Oxford, 1913, 2:20), and the Book of Enoch 6–10 (ibid., 191–95). Tertullian's "On the Veiling of Virgins," where he concurs with Paul, is translated in *The Ante-Nicene Christian Library*, 18:154–80 (see especially 165–68 for his Pauline exegesis). These ideas about veiling persisted into the later Middle Ages and Renaissance. See Maclean, *The Renaissance Notion of Woman*, section 2.8.1 and passim. Paul's admonition that males pray *without* their heads covered is, of course, anti-Jewish propaganda.

24. Kessler, *Illustrated Bibles from Tours*, 22 n. 34, notes a Syriac commentary on Genesis that indicates that God taught Eve the art of weaving.

25. Tertullian, *The Ante-Nicene Christian Library*, 11:304–5 and 309; these passages are discussed by R. H. Bloch, "Medieval Misogyny," *Representations* 20 (1987): 11–15; idem, *Medieval Misogyny and the Invention of Western Romantic Love*, Chicago and London, 1991, 39–47; and Prusak, "Woman: Seductive Siren and Source of Sin?" 104–5.

26. Miles, *Carnal Knowing*, 35 and n. 54, citing J. Z. Smith, "The Garments of Shame," 235.

27. Camille, *Gothic Idol*, 223, discusses this aspect of medieval optical theory, which is also the source for the convention of profile heads' being used for evil figures in images. Petrarch, in the fourteenth century, makes use of the poetic convention of "love's fatal glance" (discussed with further references in P. Simons, "Women in Frames: The Gaze, the Eye, the Profile in Renaissance Portraiture," in *The Expanding Discourse: Feminism and Art History*, ed. N. Broude and M. D. Garrard, New York, 1992, 50 and n. 88). The writer of the Book of Reuben acknowledges the danger of the gaze and connects it to the successful beguiling of men by women. Women, because they have "no power or strength over man, use wiles by outward attractions" and by the

"glance of the eye instill the poison" in men (Charles, *The Apocrypha and Pseudepigrapha of the Old Testament*, 1:297).

28. A general treatment of antimarriage literature and its revival in the twelfth century is found in K. M. Wilson and E. M. Makowski, *Wykked Wyves and the Woes of Marriage: Misogamous Literature from Juvenal to Chaucer*, Albany, N.Y., 1990.

29. This and the following quotation are from B. Cecchetti, "La donna nel medioevo a Venezia," *Archivio veneto* 31 (1886): 63–64. Many of Fra' Paolino's complaints—particularly those that take the formulation of "if she's such and such," that is bad, "if she's the opposite," that is even worse—come from the fragmentary *Liber aureolus de nuptiis*, attributed to Theophrastus (d. 287 B.C.E.) and preserved only in Jerome's *Adversus Jovinianum*. An English translation of it is included in R. P. Miller, ed., *Chaucer: Sources and Backgrounds*, New York, 1977, 411–14, and Wilson and Makowski discuss it in *Wykked Wyves*, 51–53 and passim.

30. *On the Misery of the Human Condition*, 17 (Dietz trans., 20–21).

31. Ibid., 20.

32. Cecchetti, "La donna nel medioevo a Venezia," 64.

33. For example, women were punished more severely for some sex crimes, such as abducting young women against their wills, yet were not regularly tried for acts of fornication and adultery. G. Ruggiero, "Sexual Criminality in the Early Renaissance: Venice 1338–1358," *Journal of Social History* 8 (1975): 21–24, discusses these and suggests that in the former case it is because those crimes were more outside the norms for female behavior, and in the latter, possibly because discipline was left to the woman's father and/or husband. It may also be that fornication and adultery were seen as "natural" for women.

34. M. M. Newett, "The Sumptuary Laws of Venice in the Fourteenth and Fifteenth Centuries," in *Historical Essays*, ed. T. F. Tout and J. Tait, London and New York, 1902, 263.

35. Many writers have noted that the thirteenth century was a time of increased repression of "others" by both the church and secular authorities. The Third and Fourth Lateran Councils of 1179 and 1215, respectively, offer examples of increased ecclesiastical controls, and many civic codes—legislating, for example, dress codes, prostitution, Jews, and Muslims—originated at this time. General treatments of this topic include Boswell, *Christianity, Social Tolerance, and Homosexuality*, 269–354; G. Duby, ed., *Revelations of the Medieval World*, vol. 2 of *A History of Private Life*, trans. A. Goldhammer, Cambridge, Mass., and London, 1988, 569–70; and J. K. Hyde, "Contemporary Views on Faction and Civil Strife in Thirteenth- and Fourteenth-Century Italy," in *Violence and Civil Disorder in Italian Cities, 1200–1500*, ed. L. Martines, Berkeley and Los Angeles, 1972, 273–307. Regarding Venetian expansion of

sumptuary legislation, rules made by men and generally aimed at controlling women, consult Newett, "The Sumptuary Laws of Venice," as well as C. Diehl, *Une république patricienne. Venise*, Paris, 1938, 151–53, where he notes Venice's reputation as a city of easy virtue. J. Herald, *Renaissance Dress in Italy, 1400–1500*, London, 1981, 161, points out that while both men and women used embellishments and perfumes, sumptuary legislation represented laws issued by men against women. Furthermore, the general ineffectiveness of the legislation is suggested by the repeated attempts to limit dress.

36. D. Herlihy, "Women and the Sources of Medieval History: The Towns of North Italy," in *Medieval Women and the Sources of Medieval History*, ed. J. T. Rosenthal, Athens, Ga., and London, 1990, 136. E. C. Dargan, *A History of Preaching*, 2 vols., New York, 1905, 1: chap. 7, gives an overview of thirteenth-century preaching and the increasing popularity of vernacular sermons. Popular preachers would often sermonize outdoors, in front of churches and in piazzas, and would make use of extra-biblical legends, folktales, and local customs as well as the standard older authorities, especially Augustine (1:187–91).

37. In the remaining Old Testament mosaics, God generally appears in the form of his gesturing right hand and almost never again in fully anthropomorphic form. The Byzantine Octateuch tradition also avoids a fully anthropomorphic Creator, similarly substituting his hand. The mosaic of Cain's conception omits even the hand and thus remains faithful to its Cotton Genesis model. It, of course, had no need for an image of the Deity, since the Genesis text makes no reference to him.

38. *Historia scholastica*, chap. 10 (PL 198:1064); see Evans, *"Paradise Lost" and the Genesis Traditions*, 169.

39. Howard, in his introduction to the translation, discusses Innocent's attack on the Cathars and his ambivalence with regard to procreation (xviii–xx). Both E. Clark, "Heresy, Asceticism, Adam, and Eve: Interpretations of Genesis 1–3 in the Later Latin Fathers," in *Genesis 1–3 in the History of Exegesis*, ed. G. A. Robbins, Lewiston, N.Y., and Queenston, Ont., 1988, 99–103, and Schreiner, "Eve, the Mother of History," passim and 151–56, discuss the conflicts inherent in medieval commentary on this divine exhortation, and Evans, 169, notes that Comestor specifically responds to the heretics on this point. E. M. Makowski, "The Conjugal Debt and Medieval Canon Law," in *Equally in God's Image*, ed. J. B. Holloway, C. S. Wright, and J. Bechtold, New York, 1990, 129–43, discusses canonical doctrine about marital sexual relations from the twelfth through mid-fourteenth centuries.

40. *On the Misery of the Human Condition*, 3 (Dietz trans., 8).

41. Silver and Smith, "Carnal Knowledge: The Late Engravings of Lucas van Leyden," 257–58.

42. See Weitzmann and Kessler, *The Cotton Genesis*, figs. 67 and 68 and text p. 58. In the badly damaged Cotton Genesis miniature, Adam's left arm crosses his chest and may reach over to Eve's breast; however, her hand does not touch Adam's genital region.

43. E. C. McLaughlin, "Equality of Souls, Inequality of Sexes," 222–33, discusses this paradox.

44. Bamberger, *Fallen Angels*, 132–34, 171, and 182, discusses some of these many stories regarding Cain. Dualists also understood Cain to be the product of evil emanations. An Ethiopic *Book of Adam and Eve* (Charlesworth, *The Old Testament Pseudepigrapha*, 2:250, identifies it as an eleventh-century Christian work based on an original composed between 100 B.C.E. and C.E. 200), popular throughout the Middle Ages, makes much of Adam and Eve's first experience of intercourse and the resultant conception of Cain, casting the event in a very positive light. According to that text, it is only after Adam and Eve marry and confirm their union that they are free of Satan's wiles. See the translation by S. C. Malan, *The Book of Adam and Eve, also Called the Conflict of Adam and Eve with Satan*, London and Edinburgh, 1882, 90–91.

45. As Weitzmann and Kessler (*The Cotton Genesis*) reconstruct the book, it included the *Birth of Cain* and the *Birth of Abel* (fol. 14r), and the *Birth of Seth* (fol. 19r) and the *Death of Adam* (fol. 20r). Both of Eve's omitted speeches use the verb *dicere*, albeit in participial form, *dicens* (saying). The first is Gen. 4:1: "dicens possedi hominem per Dominum" ("saying, I am possessed of a human through the Lord; or perhaps clearer in Hebrew, which would translate, I have gotten a man with the help of the Lord"); the second is Gen. 4:25: "dicens posuit mihi Deus semen aliud pro Abel" (saying, the Lord has appointed to me another child instead of Abel). With regard to these important speeches by Eve, discussed far less often than Gen. 1–3, see Pardes, *Countertraditions*, chap. 3, especially 52–53, where she interprets the birth of Cain (based on Eve's naming speech) as a second Fall due to pride, and that of Seth as a reconciliation between a newly rehabilitated Eve and God.

46. Demus, *Mosaics of San Marco*, 2:79.

47. The visual conventions remain important to the mosaicists. There are three additional birth scenes in the narthex mosaics. As indicated in chap. 5 n. 22 above, when Rebecca gives birth to Isaac, she lies in bed to the picture's right and her head is modestly covered. By contrast, when Hagar gives birth to Ishmael, she rests at the picture's left, her hair still uncovered and decorated with a fillet. The case of Asenath's birth of Ephraim—she is Joseph's Egyptian wife, but is in no way sinister—is more complex. Her hair modestly covered, she lies to the picture's left, while Joseph stands to the picture's right with their firstborn, Manasseh, and accepts Ephraim (Demus, *Mosaics of San Marco*,

2: pl. 292), thus demonstrating a clear sense of familial and national hierarchy.

48. Weitzmann and Kessler, *The Cotton Genesis*, 58.

49. This passage's relevance to Gen. 1–3 is discussed by J. Bassler, "Adam, Eve, and the Pastor: The Use of Genesis 2–3 in the Pastoral Epistles," in *Genesis 1–3 in the History of Exegesis*, ed. G. A. Robbins, Lewiston, N.Y., and Queenston, Ont., 1988, passim, and by Clark, "Heresy, Asceticism, Adam, and Eve," 103. Scholars today do not attribute First or Second Timothy to Paul, but he is the traditional author.

50. E. C. McLaughlin, "Equality of Souls, Inequality of Sexes," 219–21.

Chapter Six

1. See Demus, "A Renascence," 348–61.

2. Weitzmann and Kessler, *The Cotton Genesis*, 30–31, discuss the origin and date of this early Byzantine manuscript, produced, most likely, in Egypt. Demus, *Mosaics of San Marco*, 2:95, following H. Buchthal, speculates that the manuscript was brought to Venice from Alexandria. An Egyptian provenance for the manuscript would have been significant to the Venetians thanks to the translation of St. Mark's relics from Alexandria to San Marco in 829/30.

3. For Cicero's use of this rhetorical device, see *De re publica* 1.13.23 and 1.13.24–26; *Epistulae ad familiares* 1.9.10, 3.8.3, and 5.15.4; *Academicae quaestiones* 2.4.10; and *De oratore* 2.50.202. Brilliant, "The Bayeux Tapestry," 113–14, discusses the role that "HIC" plays in the Bayeux Tapestry inscription with regard to audience reception and notes that it is reserved for the most important scenes within the sequence.

4. Evans, *"Paradise Lost" and the Genesis Traditions*, 175–82, discusses this late medieval interest in divine justice.

5. D. Rosand, *"Venetia figurata:* The Iconography of a Myth," in *Interpretazioni veneziane. Studi di storia dell'arte in onore di Michelangelo Muraro*, ed. D. Rosand, Venice, 1984, 177–79. Demus, *Church of San Marco*, 14–18 and passim, also discusses the thirteenth century as a "prolific period of state-controlled mythogenesis." Additional studies on Venetian civic imagery as manifested in San Marco include Sinding-Larsen, *Christ in the Council Hall*, passim and especially 174–75 on Venice personified as virginal Justice; and Pincus, "Christian Relics and the Body Politic," 39–57.

6. Demus, *Church of San Marco*, 125–37 and 148–63, discusses the west facade and its connections to civic imagery.

7. Demus, *Mosaics of San Marco*, 2:91–93, discusses this theme. The *Judgment of Solomon* dates from the sixteenth century (ibid., 2: fig. 32), but

Demus argues that the subject is the same as in the mosaic that was there in the thirteenth century. See his fig. 26 for a view of the *Judgment* from the Creation cupola.

8. Sinding-Larsen, *Christ in the Council Hall*, 169, discusses this passage from *Ambrosius ad simplicianum*.

9. Sinding-Larsen, 167–75. These reliefs are illustrated there as pls. II and VII–XI.

10. For example, the vernacular paraphrases of Genesis produced in England and Germany in the eleventh and twelfth centuries may have been extraliturgical readings. See J. Lowden, "Concerning the Cotton Genesis and Other Illustrated Manuscripts of Genesis," *Gesta* 31 (1992): 46 n. 40.

11. O. B. Hardison, *Christian Rite and Christian Drama in the Middle Ages*, Baltimore, 1965, 88 n. 6.

12. Werckmeister, "The Lintel Fragment Representing Eve," 15–23, where he discusses the rite in general as well as the inclusion of penitential portals in medieval architecture, which he calls "common"; and Hardison, especially 87–110.

13. W. S. Gibson, "Hieronymus Bosch and the Mirror of Man," *Oud Holland* 87 (1973): 211.

14. Regarding the mirror's ability to assist the viewer to cleanse his soul, see Gibson, 218–22 and passim; and J. H. Marrow, "Symbol and Meaning in Northern European Art of the Late Middle Ages and Early Renaissance," *Simiolus* 16 (1986): 161–63, who reproduces as his fig. 18 a German woodcut of c. 1500 that juxtaposes a devil's mirror with an angel's.

15. All the other cupolas in the atrium demonstrate in a general way a wheel-like arrangement; however the Genesis cupola has a more evident structure, for it is the only one divided into multiple horizontal registers and with regular vertical divisions. Howard, in his introduction to Innocent's *On the Misery of the Human Condition* (xxiv–xxxiii), considers five chief topoi for the "contempt of the world" literature, which he categorizes as the corruption of the natural order (especially the body), the mutability of earthly things (including Fortune's Wheel and the fickleness of women), the vanity of earthly things, the evils of the social order, and punishment or reward in the afterlife. Boethius devotes the entire second book of his *De consolatione philosophiae* to Fortune, and this served as the basis for later medieval commentary on the theme. For general studies of the Fortune theme in art refer to R. van Marle, *Iconographie de l'art profane au Moyen-Age et à la Renaissance*, 2 vols., The Hague, 1931, 2:178–202; F. P. Pickering, *Literature and Art in the Middle Ages*, Coral Gables, Fla., 1970, 168–222; E. Mâle, *The Gothic Image*, New York, 1958, 94–97; Katzenellenbogen, *Allegories of*

the *Virtues and Vices*, 70–72; and E. Kitzinger, "World Map and Fortune's Wheel: A Medieval Floor Mosaic in Turin," in *Art of Byzantium and the Medieval West*, Bloomington, Ind., and London, 1976, 327–56.

16. See H. J. Dow, "The Rose-Window," *Journal of the Warburg and Courtauld Institutes* 20 (1957), especially 268–73, in addition to the works in the previous note.

17. "I reign," "I have reigned," "I am without reign," and "I shall reign." Kitzinger, "World's Map and Fortune's Wheel," 347, notes that the dominant type in the twelfth century shows Fortune standing next to the wheel and rotating it, but by the first half of the thirteenth century she more typically is located in the center of the wheel. Examples of the *regno* type can be found in the Kitzinger article and in Mâle, *Gothic Image*, 95.

18. Gregory the Great's *Moralia in Hiob*, Manchester, John Rylands Library, MS lat. 83, fol. 214v; discussed and illustrated in Pickering, *Literature and Art in the Middle Ages*, 213 and pl. 2a.

19. Kitzinger ("World's Map and Fortune's Wheel") discusses the late-twelfth-century Turin floor mosaic in the chancel of San Salvatore, noting that it conflates the circularity of Fortune's allegory with a circular *mappamundi*.

20. *Missal of Henry de Midel*, Hildesheim, c. 1159; formerly in Mülheim, Collection Count Fürstenberg-Stammheim. See H. Swarzenski, *Monuments of Romanesque Art*, 2d ed., London, 1974, 78–79, illustrated as his pl. 207, figs. 479 and 480.

21. Pickering, *Literature and Art in the Middle Ages*, 215. Of the three Fates, Clotho generally holds the distaff. See G. M. Gibson on this classical theme, "The Thread of Life in the Hand of the Virgin," 48–49, as well as O. Brendel, *The Symbolism of the Sphere*, Leiden, 1977, 50–66 and chap. 5. In the ancient world, the distaff was often accompanied by a mirror. Gibson (n. 16) recognizes that the spinning theme again identifies Eve as an antitype to the Virgin Mary, and that opposites can be cured by contraries.

22. There is a sculpture of Fortune at San Marco. Demus, *Church of San Marco*, 112 and 181–82, identifies a relief of a standing female on the north facade of San Marco as Tyche, a personification of the fortunes of Venice and the local guardian of the city's good fortune. A crowned figure, she holds a circular object in her right hand and a branching form in the left; Demus identifies these as a wreath and a cornucopia. Venice's fortunes fluctuated a great deal in the thirteenth century, and so this inclusion of a largely secular theme of Fortune within the religious setting is not surprising.

Selected References

For an extensive bibliography on the church and mosaics of San Marco, consult Otto Demus, The Mosaics of San Marco in Venice, 2 vols., Chicago and London, 1984.

Adam, a Religious Play of the Twelfth Century. Trans. Edward N. Stone. Seattle, 1928.

Alexander, Jonathan. "*Labeur* and *Paresse:* Ideological Representations of Medieval Peasant Labor." *Art Bulletin* 72 (1990): 436–52.

Allen, Prudence. *The Concept of Woman: The Aristotelian Revolution, 750 B.C.– A.D. 1250.* Montreal and London, 1985.

Alter, Robert. *The Art of Biblical Narrative.* New York, 1981.

Aschkenasy, Nehama. *Eve's Journey.* Philadelphia, 1986.

Augustine of Hippo. *The City of God by St. Augustine.* Trans. Marcus Dods. New York, 1950.

———. *St. Augustine, the Literal Meaning of Genesis.* Trans. John Hammond. Ancient Christian Writers Series, nos. 41–42. Ramsey, N.J., 1982.

Bal, Mieke. "Sexuality, Sin, and Sorrow: The Emergence of Female Character (A Reading of Genesis 1–3)." In *The Female Body in Western Culture: Contemporary Perspectives*, ed. Susan Suleiman, 317–38. Cambridge, Mass., and London, 1986.

———. *Lethal Love: Feminist Literary Readings of Biblical Love Stories.* Bloomington and Indianapolis, 1987.

Bamberger, Bernard J. *Fallen Angels.* Philadelphia, 1952.

Barasch, Moshe. *Gestures of Despair in Medieval and Early Renaissance Art.* New York, 1976.

Barr, Jane. "The Influence of St. Jerome on Medieval Attitudes to Women." In *After Eve: Women in the Theology of the Christian Tradition*, ed. Janet Martin Soskice, 89–102. London, 1990.

———. "The Vulgate Genesis and Jerome's Attitude towards Women" (1982). In *Equally in God's Image*, ed. Julia Holloway, Constance S. Wright, and Joan Bechtold, 122–28. New York, 1990.

Bassler, Jouette. "Adam, Eve, and the Pastor: The Use of Genesis 2–3 in the Pastoral Epistles." In *Genesis 1–3 in the History of Exegesis*, ed. Gregory A. Robbins, 43–65. Lewiston, N.Y., and Queenston, Ont., 1988.

Bäuml, Franz H. "Varieties and Consequences of Medieval Literacy and Illiteracy." *Speculum* 55 (1980): 237–65.

Beck, Jonathan. "Genesis, Sexual Antagonism, and the Defective Couple of the Twelfth-Century *Jeu d'Adam.*" *Representations* 29 (1990): 124–44.

Bernabò, Massimo. "La cacciata dal Paradiso e il lavoro dei progenitori in alcune miniature medievali." In *Congresso di storia della miniatura italiana. Atti del I Congresso, Cortona, 1978. La miniatura italiana in età romanica e gotica*, 269–81. Florence, 1979.

Bertoli, Bruno. *I mosaici di San Marco*. Milan, 1986.

Bettini, Sergio. *Mosaici antichi di San Marco a Venezia*. Bergamo, 1944.

Bloch, R. Howard. "Medieval Misogyny." *Representations* 20 (1987): 1–24.

———. *Medieval Misogyny and the Invention of Western Romantic Love*. Chicago and London, 1991.

Bloom, Harold. *The Book of J*. With trans. by David Rosenberg. New York, 1990.

Blum, Pamela Z. "The Cryptic Creation Cycle in Ms. Junius xi." *Gesta* 15 (1976): 211–26.

Borsook, Eve. *Messages in Mosaic*. Oxford, 1990.

Boswell, John. *Christianity, Social Tolerance, and Homosexuality*. Chicago and London, 1980.

Brendel, Otto. *The Symbolism of the Sphere*. Leiden, 1977.

Brilliant, Richard. *Visual Narratives: Storytelling in Etruscan and Roman Art*. Ithaca, N.Y., and London, 1984.

———. "The Bayeux Tapestry: A Stripped Narrative for Their Eyes and Ears." *Word and Image* 7 (1991): 98–126.

Brown, Peter. *The Body and Society: Men, Women, and Sexual Renunciation in Early Christianity*. New York, 1988.

Cadden, Joan. *Meanings of Sex Difference in the Middle Ages: Medicine, Science, and Culture*. Cambridge and New York, 1993.

Camille, Michael. "The Book of Signs: Writing and Visual Difference in Gothic Manuscript Illumination." *Word and Image* 1 (1985): 133–48.

———. "Seeing and Reading: Some Visual Implications of Medieval Literacy and Illiteracy." *Art History* 8 (1985): 26–49.

———. "The Language of Images in Medieval England, 1200–1400." In *The Age of Chivalry*, ed. John Alexander and Paul Binski, 33–40. London, 1987.

———. *The Gothic Idol: Ideology and Image-Making in Medieval Art.* Cambridge, 1989.

———. "Visual Signs of the Sacred Page: Books in the *Bible moralisée.*" *Word and Image* 5 (1989): 111–30.

Caxton, William. *The Golden Legend or Lives of the Saints as Englished by William Caxton.* 7 vols. London, 1922.

Cecchetti, Bartolomeo. "La donna nel medioevo a Venezia." *Archivio veneto* 31 (1886): 33–69 and 307–49.

———. *La vita dei veneziani nel 1300. Le vesti.* 1886. Reprint, Bologna, 1980.

Charles, R. H., ed. *The Apocrypha and Pseudepigrapha of the Old Testament in English.* 2 vols. Oxford, 1913.

Charlesworth, James H., ed. *The Old Testament Pseudepigrapha.* 2 vols. Garden City, N.Y., 1983 and 1985.

Clark, Elizabeth. "Heresy, Asceticism, Adam, and Eve: Interpretations of Genesis 1–3 in the Later Latin Fathers." In *Genesis 1–3 in the History of Exegesis*, ed. Gregory A. Robbins, 99–133. Lewiston, N.Y., and Queenston, Ont., 1988.

Comestor, Peter. *Historia scholastica.* In J. P. Migne, *Patrologiae cursus completus.* Series latina, vol. 198, 1049–1722. Paris, 1844–64.

Couffignal, Robert. *Le drame de l'Eden. Le récit de la Genèse et sa fortune littéraire.* Toulouse, 1980.

D'Alverny, Marie-Thérèse. "Les anges et les jours." *Cahiers archéologiques* 9 (1957): 271–300.

D'Angelo, Mary Rose. "The Garden: Once and Not Again. Traditional Interpretations of Genesis 1:26–17 [*sic*] in I Corinthians 11:7–12." In *Genesis 1–3 in the History of Exegesis*, ed. Gregory A. Robbins, 1–41. Lewiston, N.Y., and Queenston, Ont., 1988.

Dargan, Edwin C. *A History of Preaching.* 2 vols. New York, 1905.

Davis, Natalie Zemon. *Society and Culture in Early Modern France.* Stanford, Calif., 1975.

Demus, Otto. "A Renascence of Early Christian Art in Thirteenth-Century Venice." in *Late Classical and Mediaeval Studies in Honor of Albert Mathias Friend, Jr.*, ed. Kurt Weitzmann, 348–61. Princeton, 1955.

———. *The Church of San Marco in Venice.* Washington, D.C., 1960.

———. *The Mosaics of San Marco in Venice.* 2 vols. Chicago and London, 1984.

Diebold, William J. "Verbal, Visual, and Cultural Literacy in Medieval Art: Word and Image in the Psalter of Charles the Bald." *Word and Image* 8 (1992): 89–99.

Diehl, Charles. *Une république patricienne. Venise.* Paris, 1938.

Duby, Georges, ed. *Rivelations of the Medieval World.* Vol. 2 of *A History of Private Life.* Trans. Arthur Goldhammer. Cambridge, Mass., and London, 1988.

Duggan, Lawrence G. "Was Art Really the 'Book of the Illiterate'?" *Word and Image* 5 (1989): 227–51.

Esche, S. *Adam und Eva, Sündenfall und Erlösung.* Düsseldorf, 1957.

Evans, John Martin. *"Paradise Lost" and the Genesis Traditions.* Oxford, 1968.

Garnier, François. *Le langage de l'image au Moyen Age.* 2d ed. Paris, 1982.

Garrison, E. B. *Studies in the History of Mediaeval Italian Painting.* 4 vols. Florence, 1953–62.

Gibson, Gail McMurray. "The Thread of Life in the Hand of the Virgin." In *Equally in God's Image,* ed. Julia B. Holloway, Constance S. Wright, and Joan Bechtold, 46–54. New York, 1990.

Gibson, Walter S. "Hieronymus Bosch and the Mirror of Man." *Oud Holland* 87 (1973): 205–26.

Graves, Robert, and Raphael Patai. *Hebrew Myths: The Book of Genesis.* New York, 1964.

Green, Rosalie B. "The Adam and Eve Cycle in the *Hortus Deliciarum.*" In *Late Classical and Mediaeval Studies in Honor of Albert Mathias Friend, Jr.,* ed. Kurt Weitzmann, 340–47. Princeton, 1955.

Guldan, Ernst. *Eva und Maria.* Graz and Cologne, 1966.

Gurewich, Vladimir. "Observations on the Iconography of the Wound in Christ's Side, with Special Reference to Its Position." *Journal of the Warburg and Courtauld Institutes* 20 (1957): 358–62.

al-Hamdani, Betty A. "The Iconographical Sources for the Genesis Frescoes Once Found in S. Paolo, f.l.m." In *Atti del IX Congresso internazionale di archeologia cristiana, Rome, 1975,* 2:11–35. 2 vols. Vatican City, 1978.

Hardison, O. B. *Christian Rite and Christian Drama in the Middle Ages.* Baltimore, 1965.

Herlihy, David. "Women and the Sources of Medieval History: The Towns of North Italy." In *Medieval Women and the Sources of Medieval History,* ed. Joel T. Rosenthal, 133–54. Athens, Ga., and London, 1990.

Hieatt, A. Kent. "Eve as Reason in a Tradition of Allegorical Interpretations of the Fall." *Journal of the Warburg and Courtauld Institutes* 43 (1980): 221–26.

Higgins, Jean M. "The Myth of Eve: The Temptress." *Journal of the American Academy of Religion* 44 (1976): 639–47.

Hodges, Laura F. "Noe's Wife: Type of Eve and Wakefield Spinner." In *Equally in God's Image,* ed. Julia B. Holloway, Constance S. Wright, and Joan Bechtold, 30–39. New York, 1990.

Hoffeld, Jeffrey M. "Adam's Two Wives." *Metropolitan Museum of Art, Bulletin* 26 (1968): 430–40.

Innocent III (Lotario dei Segni). *On the Misery of the Human Condition: De miseria humanae conditionis.* Ed. Donald R. Howard, trans. Margaret M. Dietz. Indianapolis and New York, 1969.

Iversen, Margaret. "Vicissitudes of the Visual Sign." *Word and Image* 6 (1990): 212–16.

Josephus, Flavius. *The Works of Flavius Josephus.* Trans. W. Whiston. Hart-
    ford, Conn., 1919.

Katzenellenbogen, Adolf. *Allegories of the Virtues and Vices in Mediaeval Art.*
    London, 1939.

Kelly, Henry Ansgar. "The Metamorphoses of the Eden Serpent during the
    Middle Ages and Renaissance." *Viator* 2 (1971): 301–27.

Kessler, Herbert L. "An Eleventh-Century Ivory Plaque from South Italy
    and the Cassinese Revival." *Jahrbuch der Berliner Museen* 8 (1966):
    67–95.

———. "*Hic Homo Formatur:* The Genesis Frontispieces of the Carolingian
    Bibles." *Art Bulletin* 53 (1971): 143–60.

———. *The Illustrated Bibles from Tours.* Princeton, 1977.

———. "Reading Ancient and Medieval Art." *Word and Image* 5, no. 1
    (1989): 1.

Kirchner, J. *Die Darstellung des ersten Menschenpaares in der bildenden Kunst.*
    Stuttgart, 1903.

Kirschbaum, E. "L'angelo rosso e l'angelo turchino." *Rivista di archeologia
    cristiana* 17 (1940): 209–48.

Kitzinger, Ernst. "World Map and Fortune's Wheel: A Medieval Floor Mo-
    saic in Turin." In *Art of Byzantium and the Medieval West,* 327–56.
    Bloomington, Ind., and London, 1976.

Kosmer, Ellen. "The 'noyous humoure of lecherie.'" *Art Bulletin* 57 (1975):
    1–8.

Kraus, Henry. "Eve and Mary." In *Living Theatre of Medieval Art,* 41–62.
    Bloomington, Ind., 1967.

Kupfer, Marcia. *Romanesque Wall Painting in Central France: The Politics of
    Narrative.* New Haven and London, 1993.

Lavin, Marilyn Aronberg. *The Place of Narrative: Mural Decoration in Italian
    Churches, 431–1600.* Chicago and London, 1990.

Lemay, Helen Rodnite. "Some Thirteenth- and Fourteenth-Century Lec-
    tures on Female Sexuality." *International Journal of Women's Studies* 1
    (1978): 391–400.

Lewis, Suzanne. "A Byzantine 'Virgo militans' at Charlemagne's Court."
    Viator 11 (1980): 71–93.

Lowden, John. "Concerning the Cotton Genesis and Other Illustrated
    Manuscripts of Genesis." *Gesta* 31 (1992): 40–53.

Lutz, Jules, and P. Perdrizet. *Speculum humanae salvationis. Traduction inédite
    de Jean Miélot (1448).* 2 vols. Leipzig, 1907.

McLaughlin, Eleanor C. "Equality of Souls, Inequality of Sexes: Woman in
    Medieval Theology." In *Religion and Sexism,* ed. Rosemary Radford
    Ruether, 213–16. New York, 1974.

McLaughlin, Mary Martin. "Peter Abelard and the Dignity of Women:
    Twelfth-Century 'Feminism' in Theory and Practice." In *Pierre Abé-
    lard, Pierre le Vénérable. Les courants philosophiques, littéraires et artistiques*

en occident au milieu du XIIe siècle (Colloques internationaux du Centre national de la recherche scientifique, Cluny, 1972), 287–334. Paris, 1975.

Maclean, Ian. *The Renaissance Notion of Woman*. Cambridge, 1980.

Makowski, Elizabeth M. "The Conjugal Debt and Medieval Canon Law." In *Equally in God's Image*, ed. Julia B. Holloway, Joan Bechtold, and Constance S. Wright, 129–43. New York, 1990.

Malan, S. C. *The Book of Adam and Eve, also Called the Conflict of Adam and Eve with Satan*. London and Edinburgh, 1882.

Mâle, Emile. *The Gothic Image*. New York, 1958.

Markow, Deborah. "The Iconography of the Soul in Medieval Art." Ph.D. diss., New York University, 1985.

Marle, Raimond van. *Iconographie de l'art profane au Moyen-Age et à la Renaissance*. 2 vols. The Hague, 1931.

Marrow, James H. "Symbol and Meaning in Northern European Art of the Late Middle Ages and Early Renaissance." *Simiolus* 16 (1986): 150–69.

Mellinkoff, Ruth. "Riding Backwards: Theme of Humiliation and Symbol of Evil." *Viator* 4 (1973): 153–76.

Miles, Margaret R. *Carnal Knowing: Female Nakedness and Religious Meaning in the Christian West*. Boston, 1989.

Molmenti, Pompeo. *La vie privée à Venise*. Venice, 1895.

———. *Venice: Its Individual Growth from the Earliest Beginnings to the Fall of the Republic*. Pt. 1, *The Middle Ages*. 2 vols. Bergamo, 1906.

Morey, James H. "Peter Comestor, Biblical Paraphrase, and the Medieval Popular Bible." *Speculum* 68 (1993): 6–35.

Newett, M. Margaret. "The Sumptuary Laws of Venice in the Fourteenth and Fifteenth Centuries." In *Historical Essays*, ed. T. F. Tout and James Tait, 245–78. London and New York, 1902.

O'Reilly, Jennifer. *Studies in the Iconography of the Virtues and Vices*. Ph.D. diss., University of Nottingham, 1972; Garland Reprint, 1988.

Pagels, Elaine. *Adam, Eve, and the Serpent*. New York, 1988.

Palol, P. de. "Une broderie catalane d'époque romane. La Genèse de Gérone." *Cahiers archéologiques* 8 (1956): 175–214 and 9 (1957): 219–51.

Pardes, Ilana. *Countertraditions in the Bible: A Feminist Approach*. Cambridge, Mass., and London, 1992.

Pellegrino, Michele. "Il 'topos' della 'status rectus' nel contesto filosofico e biblico." In *Mullus. Festschrift Theodor Klauser*, 273–81. Vol. 1 of *Jahrbuch für Antike und Christentum*, Münster, 1964.

Phillips, John A. *Eve: The History of an Idea*. New York, 1984.

Pickering, F. P. *Literature and Art in the Middle Ages*. Coral Gables, Fla., 1970.

Pincus, Deborah. "Christian Relics and the Body Politic: A Thirteenth-Century Relief Plaque in the Church of San Marco." In *Interpretazioni veneziane. Studi di storia dell'arte in onore di Michelangelo Muraro*, ed. David Rosand, 39–57. Venice, 1984.

Prusak, Bernard P. "Woman: Seductive Siren and Source of Sin? Pseudepigraphal Myth and Christian Origins." In *Religion and Sexism*, ed. Rosemary Radford Ruether, 89–116. New York, 1974.

Rosand, David. "*Venetia figurata:* The Iconography of a Myth." In *Interpretazioni veneziane. Studi di storia dell'arte in onore di Michelangelo Muraro*, ed. David Rosand, 177–96. Venice, 1984.

Ruether, Rosemary Radford, ed. *Religion and Sexism*. New York, 1974.

Ruggiero, Guido. "Sexual Criminality in the Early Renaissance: Venice 1338–1358." *Journal of Social History* 8 (1975): 18–37.

Russell, H. Diane. *Eva/Ave: Woman in Renaissance and Baroque Prints*. Washington and New York, 1990.

Russell, Jeffrey B. *The Devil: Perceptions of Evil from Antiquity to Primitive Christianity*. Ithaca, N.Y., and London, 1977.

———. *Satan: The Early Christian Tradition*. Ithaca, N.Y., and London, 1981.

———. *Lucifer: The Devil in the Middle Ages*. Ithaca, N.Y., and London, 1984.

Schiller, Gertrude. *Iconography of Christian Art*. Trans. Janet Seligman. 2 vols. Greenwich, Conn., 1971.

Schmitt, Jean-Claude. "Introduction and General Bibliography." In *Gestures*, ed. Jean-Claude Schmitt. *History and Anthropology* 1 (1984): 1–23.

———. *La raison des gestes dans l'occident médiéval*. Paris, 1990.

———. "The Rationale of Gestures in the West: Third to Thirteenth Centuries." In *A Cultural History of Gesture*, ed. Jan Bremmer and Herman Roodenburg, 59–70. Ithaca, N.Y., 1992.

Schreiner, Susan E. "Eve, the Mother of History: Reaching for the Reality of History in Augustine's Later Exegesis of Genesis." In *Genesis 1–3 in the History of Exegesis*, ed. Gregory A. Robbins, 135–86. Lewiston, N.Y., and Queenston, Ont., 1988.

Schubert, Ursula. "Eine jüdische Vorlage für die Darstellung der Erschaffung des Menschen in der sogenannten Cotton-Genesis-Rezension?" In *Atti del IX Congresso internazionale di archeologia cristiana, Rome, 1975*, 1:433–49. 2 vols., Vatican City, 1978.

Schuyler, Jane. "The Left Side of God: A Reflection of Cabala in Michelangelo's Genesis Scenes." *Source* 6 (1986): 12–19.

———. "The Female Holy Spirit (*Shekhinah*) in Michelangelo's *Creation of Adam*." *Studies in Iconography* 11 (1987): 111–36.

Silver, Larry, and Susan Smith. "Carnal Knowledge: The Late Engravings of Lucas van Leyden." *Nederlands Kunsthistorisch Jaarboek* 29 (1978): 239–98.

Simons, Patricia. "Women in Frames: The Gaze, the Eye, the Profile in Renaissance Portraiture." In *The Expanding Discourse: Feminism and Art History*, ed. Norma Broude and Mary D. Garrard, 39–58. New York, 1992.

Sinding-Larsen, Staale. *Christ in the Council Hall: Studies in the Religious Iconography of the Venetian Republic*. Rome, 1974.

Smith, Jonathan Z. "The Garments of Shame." *History of Religions* 5 (1966): 217–38.

Smith, Susan L. "'To Women's Wiles I Fell': The Power of Women *Topos* and the Development of Medieval Secular Art." Ph.D. diss., University of Pennsylvania, 1978.

———. "The Power of Women *Topos* on a Fourteenth-Century Embroidery." *Viator* 21 (1990): 203–28.

———. *The Power of Women.* Philadelphia, 1995.

Steinberg, Leo. "Eve's Idle Hand." *Art Journal* 35 (1975–76): 130–35.

———. "The Line of Fate." *Critical Inquiry* 6 (1980): 411–54.

Tertullian. Vols. 11, 15, and 18 in *The Ante-Nicene Christian Library.* Eds. Alexander Roberts and James Donaldson. 24 vols. Edinburgh, 1868–72.

Trible, Phyllis. "Depatriarchalizing in Biblical Interpretation" (1973). In *The Jewish Woman: New Perspectives,* ed. Elizabeth Koltun, 217–40. New York, 1976.

Weitzmann, Kurt. "The Genesis Mosaics of San Marco and the Cotton Genesis Miniatures." In Otto Demus, *The Mosaics of San Marco in Venice,* 2:105–42. 2 vols. Chicago and London, 1984.

Weitzmann, Kurt, and Herbert Kessler. *The Cotton Genesis.* Princeton, 1986.

Werckmeister, O. K. "The Lintel Fragment Representing Eve from Saint-Lazare, Autun." *Journal of the Warburg and Courtauld Institutes* 35 (1972): 1–30.

Williams, John. "*Generationes Abrahae:* Reconquest Iconography in Leon." *Gesta* 16 (1977): 3–14.

Wilson, Adrian, and Joyce Lancaster Wilson. *A Medieval Mirror: Speculum humanae salvationis, 1324–1500.* Berkeley, Los Angeles, London, 1984.

Wilson, Katharina M., and Elizabeth M. Makowski. *Wykked Wyves and the Woes of Marriage: Misogamous Literature from Juvenal to Chaucer.* Albany, N.Y., 1990.

Wolfthal, Diane. "'A Hue and a Cry': Medieval Rape Imagery and Its Transformation." *Art Bulletin* 75 (1993): 39–64.

Illustration Credits

Author: Figs. 1, 2, 3, 11; Alinari/Art Resource, New York: Figs. 4, 13, 18, 27; Courtesy of the Bayerische Staatsbibliothek, Munich: Fig. 32; Biblioteca Vaticana: Fig. 17; Bibliothèque nationale, Paris: Fig. 29; By permission of The British Library: Plate 12, Figs. 30, 33; Dumbarton Oaks, Washington, D.C., © 1996: Plates 1, 2, 3, 4, 5, 6, 7, 11; Courtesy of the Photographic Archives of the National Gallery of Art, Washington, D.C.: Figs. 5, 6, 7, 8, 9, 10, 12, 14, 19, 20, 21, 22, 23, 24, 25, 26, 28, 31; The Pierpont Morgan Library, © 1996: Plate 8; Scala/Art Resource, New York: Plates 9, 10; Universitätsbibliothek Salzburg: Figs. 15, 16

Index

Designer: Janet Wood
Compositor: G & S Typesetters, Inc.
Text: 10.5/15 Janson
Display: Janson
Printer: Data Reproductions
Binder: Roswell